A Rainbow Book

One Can Do It

A How-To Guide for the Physically Handicapped

written & illustrated by
Sheri Coin Marshall

Rainbow Books, Inc.

Library of Congress Cataloging-in-Publication Data

Marshall, Sheri Coin, 1953–
    One can do it : a how-to guide for the physically handicapped /
Sheri Coin Marshall ; illustrations, Sheri Coin Marshall.
        p.   cm.
    ISBN 1-56825-002-9 : $14.95
    1. Physically handicapped–United States–Biography.
2. Physically handicapped–United States–Life skills guides.
 I. Title.
HV3013.M37A3   1993
362.4'092–dc20
    [B]   93-22307
                                                              CIP

One Can Do It:
A How-To Guide for the Physically Handicapped

Copyright © 1994 by Sheri Coin Marshall
Cover & Interior Design: Betsy Lampé
Cover Photo: Joe C. Marshall, III
Published by Rainbow Books, Inc.
    P. O. Box 430
    Highland City, FL 33846-0430
    Telephone: (813) 648-4420

This book has been set in 14-point type for the visually impaired. Information included does not substitute for or preclude the advice of a physician or medical experts.

Manufactured in the United States of America.

Dedication

To my mother, Phyllis Vogler, my father, Richard Coin, my brother, Brian Coin and my husband, Joe C. Marshall, III. Their assistance, positive thoughts and optimistic outlook on life encouraged me to try the impossible. Their loving support and encouragement have been invaluable.

Contents

Acknowledgments

I would like to thank to the following individuals for their assistance with this book:

Mary O' Dell, Green River Writers
Jim Van Buskirk
Shirley Horger
Paul E. Kauffman

Without their professional editing skills and support, I would never have completed this project.

Preface

I began to write this book after I received a letter from an acquaintance, Leah. In her letter, Leah, in her early twenties, explained that she had a large, cancerous tumor on the bone of her right upper arm. She was being given medication in an attempt to shrink the tumor, she explained. But in the meantime, the pain was extremely intense. The outcome of the medication was uncertain, and she was convinced her arm would be amputated. She actually expressed a *desire* to have her arm amputated so she could be relieved of the pain, the mental stress, and so she could get on with her life.

She asked me how she might prepare herself for her potential loss. There were questions such as, "How will people judge my appearance? Will they stare? What about clothing? Dressing myself? Everyday tasks? Driving? Preparing meals?"

I began to write to her and realized I had so much to say. There was abundant background information to share. There were so many ways I had dealt successfully with routine tasks. During my quest to set and achieve specific goals, I had triumphed over my impairment. I had completed the unimaginable, the seemingly impossible.

Before long, I realized she was not an isolated case. I began to notice on daily news broadcasts that there were many individuals suffering traumatic amputations or the loss of the use of a limb.

They need to know they are not alone and that life *does* continue.

Introduction

The first time I met Sheri, 25 years ago, I was dressed as Moses from *The Ten Commandments*, holding cardboard tablets covered with Hebrew characters copied from the *World Book Encyclopedia*. My outfit was based on Charlton Heston's from the front cover of the sound-track album and sewn up by my mother. Sandals bought especially for the costume, and which I wore for years after, became known as the Moses sandals. My hair, in its permanent pompadour, was sprayed with silver hairspray. At the Halloween dance, a friend pointed out a fat lady with an enormous chest and butt, and suggested I ask her to dance. Sure, why not? We won third prize for best costumes.

So I almost didn't recognize her when Sheri invited me to the "Sharps and Flats Ball," sponsored by the choir and band of LaPalma Junior High. It was a big event in my circle because, though I was a member of neither musical club, all my friends seemed to be. I was surprised and flattered because I really didn't know Sheri. She was a sophomore and I was a junior. I went to Flowers by Roy to buy her a corsage — a first for me. I really didn't know what I was doing.

The night of the dance, I got dressed up and my mom drove me over to Sheri's house. Did we walk from there or did Sheri's mom drive us? I can't remember. She liked the corsage, although there was that awkward moment when I tried to pin it on. I think her mom came to the rescue just as I was about to lose it completely from nervousness. Anyway, we hit it off and started "dating."

Years before, at the Buena Park Municipal Pool — "the

plunge" — I remember having seen a girl with one arm at swimming lessons. I feared diving and was impressed that she was so good at it. It seemed odd to connect so many years later.

Our "dates" consisted of riding around on her tandem bicycle with the little pink basket in front. I was in front to steer. I always seemed to have a two-for-the-price-of-one coupon to some fast-food establishment. It seemed to me a good, inexpensive excuse for going to lunch. I later heard through the "grapevine" that Sheri made fun of me for the "coupon dates." Although it was amusing later, at the time I was devastated.

Or we'd ride over to the Sears store in the Buena Park Center Mall. I remember the time that I was buying some pants and told the clerk that they were too big and him saying, "Well, maybe your wife can take them in a bit for you." Sheri and I just looked at each other in embarrassed amusement. We must have been about 15 — how could he possibly have assumed we were husband and wife? Still, that was the assumption, that we would eventually marry, set up housekeeping and have children.

Sheri was so thoughtful. For my birthday one year she gave me a little cardboard case with three drawers. From each of the drawers I kept pulling one little package of individually wrapped gifts after another, all tied together on the same length of red ribbon — erasers, gum, box of stars, etc. I treasure the memory of the imagination and time that went into that gift. I also treasure that yellow-and-green box; it's been nearly 25 years, but I still have it.

On another birthday she took me to The Buttery for dinner. In fact, I have the photograph her mom took of us before we left. Sheri looked like Nancy Sinatra in high, white, patent-leather boots and a short, white dress with long sleeves. I was wearing maroon, grey and navy-striped "flair" pants over boots, with a double-breasted navy blazer.

When we got to the restaurant I was amazed that the host knew who we were and ushered us to a quiet corner table. After we finished the meal, with no discernible prompting from Sheri, a little cake with a candle was brought in and I was wished, "Happy Birthday." I was flabbergasted. How had all this happened?

"I came down in person to make the reservation," Sheri finally told me.

I was very impressed with her thoughtfulness and attention to detail; I'd never heard of such attention to detail. She wanted to make sure it all went right.

I remember the time shortly before our family was to move to the Pacific Northwest. It was quite a trauma for us, because we'd lived in that house for twelve years; my brother was born there. Most other kids moved around at least some, but I couldn't ever remember *not* living there. That evening we were supposed to go over to Steve Lewis'. I couldn't really figure out why — our families didn't really socialize. When I got there, Betty Lewis said that Steve was out on the patio. Sure enough, there he was surrounded by all our friends. I really *was* surprised. I kept saying, "I spent the whole day with Sheri, and she didn't say a word." I would never have been able to keep a secret so well.

Sheri was one of the few friends who came to visit while I lived near Seattle. I was so excited she was coming. We had dinner at the Space Needle, which I think may have been another "coupon date;" my mother had given me some special offer. Sheri stayed at our house, and I was amazed that she was so pleasant in the morning. Being grouchy until I am fully awake, I never knew that some people wake up sweetly.

Then there's the goofy picture of the two of us as bridesmaid and best man at Bill Morris' ill-fated wedding. Sheri looked like "Spring" in her green floor-length dress with sun hat and basket of flowers, and I wore the first dinner jacket I'd ever rented. It was just after that that we went out to a secluded field in the middle of nowhere and laid out in the sun. Something amorous was *supposed* to happen, but it didn't. I think we were both affected by the wedding of our friends, but in different ways.

I don't know exactly what we had in common, but we had some special affinity. As I think back on it, perhaps it was some sort of feeling of being "different." I always seemed to forget that she had lost her right arm in an early childhood accident — only when we posed for pictures, and she made a point of standing so that it was scarcely noticeable. She drove a stick shift, operated a PBX switchboard, played a harp, threw pottery, flew airplanes. Tell Sheri she couldn't do something, and she was already figuring out how she would accomplish it. I admired her for her determination; she always reached her goals.

My own feeling of lack of belonging was probably due to my still-budding homosexuality. At the time, neither of us understood that, and I think it may have been frustrating for both of us that the relationship did not develop as it might have. But as always, Sheri was a good sport and later met several of my boyfriends and heartily approved.

We may have seen each other infrequently over the years,

but we corresponded regularly. Our lives had gone in different directions geographically and in other ways, but we kept each other up to date; much more so than with many other friends.

Although we had not seen each other in some time, when she announced that she was marrying Joe Marshall, my partner and I made a special effort to drive to Los Angeles for the reception. It was good to see her happily married, something she'd always wanted.

Now, sitting in the house I've bought with my partner, I look at the holiday picture of Sheri with her husband and new baby and think back on all the years that have passed since "Moses and the fat lady" danced together for the first time.

Jim Van Buskirk

Part I
My Story

Chapter 1
Morning Star

Gardena, California, is one of those nondescript bedroom communities connected with many similar cities all running together on the outskirts of Los Angeles. My parents, Phyllis and Richard Coin, both in their early twenties, my brother Brian, one year of age, and I lived there in a neat, two-bedroom court apartment. From what I can recall about our surroundings from those early years, near the rear of the property, set apart from the two rows of apartments, was a community wash house. Inside were coin washers and dryers for tenants' use and also room for our family's washer plus an area to set up toys and for play. Since all the children in the court played frequently in the wash house, my parents told me later on in my childhood, they were satisfied with checking in on us occasionally, not realizing there was any danger lurking there.

The only difference about this particular day in August 1957, as I recollect, was that my friend and I decided to do a load of laundry. Covering our family's washer was a bulky bedspread which I proceeded to stuff into the washer while my friend busily turned the washer on. She quickly turned the control dial past the wash to the spin cycle. The washer tub began to spin slowly, but rapidly gained speed, twisting the bedspread around the agitator inside the drum. Suddenly I realized I couldn't pull my arm loose from the tightly twisted fabric. I remember being pulled down into the washer drum along with the bedspread. In less than a minute my arm was literally twisted off, dangling only by a pencil-size, rope-like piece of skin.

My parents heard my heart-stopping screams and ran to see what had happened. My mother immediately called an ambulance and, not knowing the extent of my injury, told me – after I was of adult age – that she had envisioned my right arm in a full-length cast. My dad stopped the washer and carefully withdrew me, along with the bedspread coiled around my mangled arm, not believing what he saw. I remember no physical pain. I was taken directly to an emergency room where the doctor on duty told my parents, "Sheri has lost her arm." In a glum tone of voice he added, "I am going to *try* to save her life."

I was given essential treatment to stabilize my condition, and then I was transported immediately by ambulance to the nearest hospital. There, a different doctor and his trauma team took me to surgery. Afterwards, I experienced a most unpleasant hospital stay.

The nurses insisted that I keep the I.V. tube positioned between my big and second toe, since it was placed in an incision at my right ankle. I would remove the tube between my toes only to have the nurses promptly replace it. The hospital environment, in general, was foreign and sterile.

Leaving the hospital, I can remember that what was left of my right arm, after the above-elbow amputation, was tingly, like it was asleep. This may have been what's referred to now as "phantom feelings." At that early age, jumping into the back seat of our car to go home, I can remember feeling a great loss. I knew something was different, and it felt so wrong. I felt empty. I imagine I was very depressed but at that age did not know what that word meant, as I do now. I was three years old.

The years after the amputation and throughout childhood were spent making trips to an orthopedic hospital near downtown Los Angeles for therapy of some sort and to the "artificial arm" makers. I never understood the trips to the orthopedic hospital. I hated the ordeal and felt dehumanized, though my parents believed that they were doing what was correct and expected for my rehabilitation.

In the early 1960s, I was poster child for the hospital. I wanted no part of this ordeal and despised photographs of myself sporting the latest prosthetic fashion. I felt exploited. I also detested visiting the "ficial arm" makers, as I referred to them. It was a dark, depressing place that smelled of burning plastic, and it was filled with crippled men who used their own devices. All and all, a very grim experience for a child.

Several times I felt overcome with the strain of having one arm and wanted desperately to have two arms like everyone else. My mother was remarkable at dealing with my outbursts. She tried to present my set of circumstances in a positive way though she knew I was terribly frustrated.

After the accident, I was given a book of Emerson by a thoughtful friend. The friend had outlined some suggested excerpts that he thought might help me later on understand my tragic loss. Some time later, and after I could read, I angrily ripped all the pages out of the leather-bound copy during one of my grieving moments. I burst into tears as I presented the destroyed book to my mother. She calmly took the book and put it away. She never scolded me for the incident nor did she ever offer the book to me again, which suited me. She was tender, understanding and helpful, and I often think how lucky I was to have her.

My dad has always had patience and persistence in the worst of situations. I fortunately inherited the same qualities from him, especially an aptitude for minute details or manipulations necessary to complete difficult or lengthy tasks. Though I struggled to accomplish tasks easy for the two-handed, I became an "overachiever" and made every project a challenge. My dad worked long hours as a steamfitter/welder, and during his days off, he was always there to help me, if I asked, with any special project.

My parents did everything within their power to provide me with a normal life style, which included typical childhood experiences. My mother taught me to tie my shoes after having to carefully rethink the task, from a two-handed to one-handed function. Both my parents showed exceptional amounts of patience when teaching me how to ride a bicycle. My mother encouraged me to develop my swimming skills. After numerous summer sessions of group lessons, I became an Advance Red Cross Swimmer.

My family could not have anticipated or ever realized how much my life and theirs would be affected by the loss of my arm. In public places they often were faced with negative looks or cold, disbelieving stares by others. My family was so happy to have me alive that we all plowed forward *together* without doubting for a minute that I was capable of accomplishing whatever I decided upon.

I never felt as if my family treated me differently because

I had one arm. Both of my parents attempted to over-compensate in the other direction, exercising a firm stand for fairness. My brother and I were treated equally with no special accommodations for my condition. I never detected that they felt guilty the accident happened, nor did I. My parents seemed to have had a healthy, positive mental outlook which included continuing forward with life instead of dwelling

Sheri, at 3 months, with parents Phyllis and Richard Coin.

on past events. This philosophy they successfully passed on to me.

I entered public school shortly after my family moved to Buena Park during the summer of 1959. I found myself doing everything everyone else did at school, and more. In kindergarten, though, other children called me Captain Hook, since my prosthetic arm had a hook that allowed me to grasp and hold objects. I opened it by twisting my torso to the right. It was awkward, but state-of-the-art in the late 1950s. It was also uncomfortably hot and became very heavy on my shoulder as the day went on, so I elected not to wear it on a daily basis. The other children's cruel remarks, so painfully honest about the arm's uncommon appearance, caused me to retreat on occasion to a storage closet outside the kindergarten room. From the closet I could hide until their attention was distracted elsewhere. Then I would peer out the cracked door, exiting only when I could safely avoid being heckled.

When I wore short-sleeved dresses without the pros- thetic arm, the children would attempt to look up my sleeve to see what remained of my arm. This embarrassed me, and I refused to let them scrutinize my body. Their curiosity made me feel like a foreign object. I felt different, because I didn't fit in with "whole" children. I wore the prosthetic arm off and on until I was about eleven.

I continued to compete with others physically, though, and remained within the norm. I also found out rather early that I was above the level of the other children when it came to mental gymnastics. At the end of the sixth grade I received one of four scholastic achievement awards given to our school and was honored at a banquet. My parents beamed as I went forward to receive my award – at the top of my class!

During the childhood years my parents were particularly fond of traveling. From the time my brother and I were toddlers our parents would take us to our grandparents' resort near Sequoia National Park. My grandparents, Clyde and Margie Johnson, had a partnership in a resort, during the mid to late 1950s, which they named Slick Rock. It was located in Three Rivers and bordered the clear, unpolluted Kaweah River. The resort offered overnight camping and day picnic facilities. The site on the river where it was located was unique. On the opposite side of the river, across from the resort, was a mountain shelled with rock that extended down below the water level of the river. The river curved at that point producing a natural eddy. The tornadic effect generated a deep green pool of water and a sandy beach on the resort side. The rock stretching into the water was

Sheri, with brother, Brian, and father, Dick, at Slick Rock in the summer of 1957.

covered with brown algae making it too slick to stand on. That is how the resort acquired its name.

Slick Rock was a spectacular place to visit, and I have many fond memories of our trips to that area. I loved the herb-filled smell of the air after sunset; the unforgettable sound of tire inner-tubes smacking the river water.

My brother and I would spend countless hours combing the beach and rocky shoreline, examining the plant and insect life. We enjoyed the warm days and cool nights during the summer months. Together we played, explored and grew closer to one another. We learned how to operate my grandfather's Ford tractor, rode the neighbor's horses and became proficient swimmers. While I was there I forgot I was physically impaired. It was a natural stress reliever. I was able to work on my physical skills, at my own pace, in the relaxed environment.

The resort eventually was condemned by the Corps of Engineers after the department decided to build a dam southwest of Three Rivers. The dam would cause the water contained below Slick

Sheri with Grandmother Margie at Slick Rock in the mid-fifties.

Rock to cover the property during peak spring thaw months. As much as the Slick Rock partnership and the community protested, the engineers went ahead with their project. The resort was officially closed in the early 1960s, and my grandparents moved to West Los Angeles.

Although Slick Rock was gone, our family continued to visit Three Rivers often. Since my father enjoyed driving, and we were bitten early on by the travel bug, we journeyed to many parts of the Southwest, Mexico, Canada and the Pacific Northwest. We included in our trips a visit to national and state parks in seven western states. We traveled to the east coast to explore New York City and see our nation's capital. We also toured the Florida Keys, spent spring break at Ft. Lauderdale and vacationed in Hawaii twice. These adventures added to my understanding of American culture. The excursions were unmatched learning experiences and caused me to become a vagabond at heart.

In the fall of 1967, I started junior high school and enjoyed new freedom and independence. I accelerated scholastically, was a member of the National Honor Society and received awards year after year. I liked the variety of classes and progressed rapidly in sewing, cooking, and other skills taught in homemaking class. I thought of myself as a professional seamstress when one of my dresses was prominently displayed in the school administration office. Until then, my mother had labored to make most of my clothes, and I mean *slaved!* It took considerable thought and planning to come up with patterns which incorporated button-up or zippered fronts so that I could dress myself. She also helped me learn to sew well, so that I could carry on a tradition handed down from her mother.

Dick, Phyllis, Brian and Sheri visiting the Car Barn, in San Francisco, in the late 1960s.

After Slick Rock closed, my grandmother, Margie Johnson, made custom clothes for wealthy and famous clients in Beverly Hills. I adored the chance to stay with Gramma Margie during school vacations. I learned to bead and work with exotic fabrics and laces, not realizing that one day I would use these skills to create a new product to patent.

I enjoyed my many friends in junior high school and realized that as we all matured, it seemed easier for them to accept me as I was. Gone were the days that my peers attempted to inspect my body.

I was attracted to Jim Van Buskirk, a student a year older than I, who I met in the cafeteria service line. We once attended a Halloween dance together, he as Moses and I as a fat lady. After this experience we became fast friends and are still close. He thought I was extremely talented and often stood in awe of how I could manage day-to-day tasks with only one arm. He introduced me to his friends, who shortly thereafter became my friends. "Our groupie," which is how we referred to ourselves, grew up sharing a variety of unforgettable experiences throughout junior and senior high school.

Jim and I continued our relationship until he and his family relocated to the Pacific Northwest before his senior year at high school. During the time we spent together, and before we could drive, we rode a tandem bicycle to the shopping mall together or to a fast food restaurant. Jim learned to drive first, since he was a year older than I was. I was excited when he, his dad and brother came by my house and picked me up for a drive. Jim was so cautious and took my kidding about his conservative driving style in good humor. Learning to drive expanded our world and lead to some typical, weekend misbehaving which included late night toilet-papering adventures.

Those friends who were popular or at the opposite end of the spectrum, woke up to a fairyland of paper streamers hung from bushes and trees. It was a challenge for our group to arrive and complete the papering quietly. We were rarely caught.

We also excelled as a group at scholastics. Jim received writing awards, Lissa and Andy, honors for outstanding grades. We all felt that being smart was not nerdy but a plus in preparing for college.

Another close friend was Freddy Jo Van Meter. Our relationship came out of necessity at first. She had polio shortly after birth, which affected her left side by making it somewhat paralyzed. Freddy walked with a limp, and her arm was slightly usable though weak. She was unable to completely stretch her arm out straight, and it always

Sheri and friend Freddy Jo Van Meter working in tandem on an archery project.

seemed to involuntarily return to the same atrophied position. Because of her palsy, she seemed to struggle so much more than I thought I did. But being with her was a mirror image of me. As we got to know each other, I realized she was extremely intelligent and quick to figure a way to do a new task, mostly one-handed. We began working together at the Brownie level of Girl Scouts at seven or eight years old. We learned archery in junior high school. She held the bow, I shot the arrow. This was newsworthy enough to make the local paper, complete with photograph. I was her left hand, she was my right, and together we accomplished what one person could. We were satisfied and happy to be reaching mutual goals. We've remained friends until today, and we still help each other tackle life's little inconveniences.

Freddy was a help to me later on when it came to handling babies. She had thoroughly researched all the one-handed baby items on the market, including furniture, cribs, high chairs, car seats and diapering methods. Because she had her daughter first, this allowed me to benefit from her baby experiences, which were invaluable.

High school was not a particularly triumphant time for

me, but I did overcome three obstacles. The first one was to insist, then to prove, that I could participate in regular, rather than adaptive, physical education classes. I had attended two years of adaptive physical education in junior high and didn't like it. I felt the other class members were being catered to, and since I had never been given any special privileges, it went against my grain. I wanted to do more and felt that I was coordinated and capable, so I convinced my teachers to let me try regular physical education. From that time forward I was able to compete successfully with others at any activity except those such as chin-ups or golf. I was expected to participate in only those sports I thought I could manage; but I was initially encouraged to try all activities. I was very competitive at softball, volleyball and swimming.

I would have also liked to have been either a cheerleader or a member of the drill team. Unfortunately, all of the routines required two hands, and it was soon obvious to me that I was neither popular enough to be a cheerleader nor equipped with the two hands it took to be part of the drill team. As much as I wanted to participate in this activity, I felt, if allowed to do so, I would look strange, only because the idea behind drill team was continuity.

It seemed during the high school years, though, there was a huge emphasis placed on body image. It bothered me that there was so much priority placed on being whole in order to participate.

My second hurdle was to convince my driver training instructor that I could, indeed, drive a car. My parents were both excellent drivers and, by applying what I had learned watching them, I found that driving came naturally. My family had confidence in my driving skills, and after getting my driver's license at age sixteen, my grandparents gave me their car, a 1957 Mercury with electric push-button transmission. It was exciting to have a car with a trunk big enough to sneak four friends into the drive-in theater.

My third challenge was to learn to throw pottery. Again, through high school, I looked for ways of allowing my creativity to show, as well as to achieve a sense of normalcy and balance in my life. I'm sure the ceramics teacher was stunned when I asked him to show me how to throw pots, but he agreed to meet me before school one morning.

As he prepared his demonstration, he said, "I'm not sure how to teach you to throw one-handed, but I will show you how I do it, and you can go from there."

At least, I thought, he didn't discourage me, which I appreciated as well as the time he spent with me on an individual basis.

I watched carefully as he took a lump of clay, placed it on the electric wheel and started it spinning. Next, he centered the lump, made an indentation in the top and pushed his thumbs into its center. Then he pulled the clay up and out from the base, shaping it into a cylinder. After slowing the wheel, he shaped the cylinder into a bowl, working with it until it reached the size and shape he wanted. Then he stopped the wheel, cut the bowl off with a potter's string and slid the finished piece onto a wood bat to dry.

Now it was my turn. I had a hard time getting the clay to center, and my first pot was a wobbly, overworked mess of saturated clay. It would take some practice, but I decided to master the clay instead of letting it master me.

For the next two weeks I went to school an hour early and

Sheri with her parents, Dick and Phyllis, before the high school graduation ceremony, June, 1971.

worked on the wheel. My persistence paid off, and after ten hours of practice, I threw my first small, perfectly centered pot. My ceramics teacher and I were equally thrilled.

I went on to eventually have a one-woman show at the public library and to sell my pots to local boutiques. It was a hobby that I never tired of. I worked to formulate my own glaze recipes and ventured into Raku and various types of stoneware, low-fire clay and glazes.

My dad made me a crude potter's wheel and helped me set up a shop in the garage with my own kiln. I was satisfied throwing pots in my informal studio for hours on end.

With some positive events happening in high school there were still negative aspects. I wanted to learn to type properly and in a professional manner. Most other high school girls were taking at least one typing class along with another business class of some sort. Freddy Jo wanted to take the typing class as well, but the teacher of the class refused to let either of us take it. His reasons, in my opinion, were unfounded. It would be necessary for him to grade us differently than the two-handed typists, and he was unwilling to do that for us. Freddy and I felt ostracized. Again, I thought about pressing the issue. Instead, I asked for a typewriter as a gift from my parents one Christmas and then taught myself to type. To hell with his silly grading format!

I desperately wanted a boyfriend during my senior year of high school and didn't have one. I wanted to attend the prom or football games on a consistent basis, but was never asked to go anywhere by any guy. During my senior year, I finally had the nerve to ask a handsome fellow that was in my pottery class to go with me to the girl-ask-guy Christmas Dance. I thought we were fairly good friends, and we at least had a common interest in pottery. He flatly refused to accompany me to the formal affair. I was crushed. I felt as if my world was crumbling as I stood there in front of him. My face felt prickly, and my head felt as if it wanted to leave my body. I was certain my having one less arm had everything to do with his decision.

From that point forward I chose to ignore the guys, skip football games and other high-school-related social activities. I concentrated on improving my pottery skills and seeing my group of junior high school friends who, by now, were all in their first year of college.

I also landed my first real job during the last semester of high school, working evenings and weekends at a Chevrolet dealership as a PBX operator/receptionist. I had gained the primary experience for this job at age 15, after working a summer job for the City of Buena Park answering the switchboard. I worked at Eddie Hopper Chevrolet for over three years and discovered that in many ways the "real" world was both better and worse than high school. On the positive side, I found out that the world of work was not a big clique, as was high school; I didn't feel I had to fit in or conform because of peer pressure. I realized the more independent and responsible I became, the more rewards there were for this type of behavior. On the other hand, I had to work harder than others to gain acceptance, to make that all-important first impression, and then continue doing my best to prove I was worthy of the job. Because of my missing limb, I was not accepted as quickly as I had been in my sheltered, high school peer group.

Work at the Chevrolet dealership, though, was never dull. For me, a naive 17 year old, the salesmen were experienced men of the world. I learned, though, as time went on that they were mostly full of bull crap. This helped me take their stories lightly, and it was entertaining.

Located in the new car showroom was the switchboard and paging system I operated. One evening during a lull, a small group of salesmen gathered around the counter next to the switchboard. They began to swap stories. Each tale became larger than the previous one. As the salesmen stood enthralled in listening and thinking about their next boastful anecdote to tell the others, I silently rotated the paging microphone around facing the desk. Undetected, I turned the system on.

They were unable to hear themselves over the paging system which was broadcasting their lively conversation over all nine acres of Eddie Hopper Chevrolet. After a few minutes, the switchboard lighted up indicating an inside call. I answered and heard the manager's voice on the other end of the line say to me, "Hon, I know it's a slow night, but will you **PLEASE** turn off that damned pager!?!"

Work at the car dealership became effortless, and college classes were easy. I continued to work on social relationships and other aspects of my life. I set goals and persisted to achieve them. I wanted independence, wanted to move out of my parents' new home in Anaheim and live on my own, buy a newer car, finish college, have a boyfriend, maybe even get married. I tested the waters, put aside unattainable goals in favor of possible ones and achieved success after success.

My dad discovered a pinhole in the engine block of the 1957 Mercury my grandparents had given me, and the aged car died soon after.

Getting to college classes and work proved to be nearly impossible without my own wheels. I needed something newer and more stimulating to drive. I searched until I found exactly what I wanted – a used 1970 Rally Sport Z/28 Camaro with a four-speed transmission. My dad, a mechanical wizard, pronounced the car sound, so we bought it. He installed power steering, which he felt was a necessity for me. In addition, he wanted to change the four-speed to an automatic transmission. I convinced him to let that project go for a while and let me try to drive the car as it was. After high school I learned to drive a stick shift and knew it demanded more planning ahead. For example, I knew to downshift to a lower gear before slowing to turn a corner. I soon developed the required smoothness and coordination. I sold the car five years later with the original four-speed transmission still remaining.

Chapter 2
Growing Up

I n fulfilling my goal to get a newer car, I achieved a greater degree of independence. Another benefit of having the Z/28 Camaro was that my brother, also a Camaro owner, and I were readily accepted into the neighborhood "Camaro Club," a group of extroverted, daredevil street racers.

Misbehaving has always been a favorite pastime of mine, if the behavior bordered on the edge of getting caught by the authorities. We spent nearly every weekend driving around town, going to any number of our splendid, Southern California beaches and street racing.

Police briefings were held at 10:30 each evening, and this was our favorite, and obviously the shrewdest, time for racing. We were loosely organized but did have several quarter-mile strips marked off around the growing city of Anaheim. The Camaro Club was a friendly, active group, and they conveniently met nearby our house. During my time with the Club, I can only remember one incident remotely related to my having one arm.

One balmy summer evening when we were together, a cocky newcomer teased me about my missing arm. He laughed and pulled at my empty sleeve. Without thinking, I popped him in the mouth, knocking him to the ground. Shocked and terribly embarrassed at my complete lack of control, I went home in tears. My brother, who has been my biggest fan and protector since childhood, reassured me that the guy had it coming after his rude, unthinking behavior. I learned something about myself during that episode — I was still vulnerable and sensitive about my arm, despite feeling accepted by the group in general.

It was through this club I met and dated several young men and eventually had a steady. Going with Rick was exciting. He was my first *serious* boyfriend! This was quite a switch from my companionless high school days. Yet, I was still puzzled by what had changed that made men more attracted to me. Was it the fact that I was dealing with the real world rather than the protected, cliquish high school mentality? After several months of dating, Rick and I fell madly in love and at one point during our turbulent, five-year, on-again, off-again relationship, considered marriage.

I continued to attend college, to work, to save money, and, at the age of 20, I decided to move out of my parents' home. Being on my own was to be a true test of my independence. Finally, I would know if I was able to survive without being under the parental umbrella.

By then I had resigned from the Chevrolet dealership and accepted a position as a full-time paste-up artist. For the time being I had decided a career as a graphic artist suited me better than a career in the food service field. Up until that time I had been pursuing a career in both areas and hadn't made a final career decision. My supervisor at the art house didn't know how I was going to cut and paste type, but I managed to do so and could keep pace with the two-handers.

I soon found a new female roommate at the art house. We'd known each other only three days before we decided to share an apartment. We were quite compatible and roomed together for several years.

Being on my own hadn't proved to be much of a struggle, and I hadn't had to compromise my living standard either. Meanwhile, Rick and I were growing further apart. He had begun to resent my fierce independence and my desire for setting and achieving goals. His possessiveness became repulsive to me, and I became attracted to other men. The final blow came when, with the help of my parents, I purchased my first house. Up until then, I hadn't undertaken anything quite so bold. I had mixed feelings about ending it with Rick, possibly because I wondered how difficult it would be to find another man who would accept me as I was. Buying the house without him, though, was *for him* the end of our relationship.

Being without Rick and in my new home, a 60-year-old frame home near downtown Orange, California, I felt like a rejuvenated person, free of bondage. I was soon wrapped up in maintaining, managing and making improvements to the house. By then I had a total of two roommates to help with monthly payments. Painting and making repairs, such as re-grouting the sink tile, were challenging to me.

I was attending a different college and working full-time as a food service supervisor at a local hospital. The new food service position was really more than I had the knowledge and skill to handle, but my boss was impressed with my college background and my attitude. He thought I would be an asset to the department, but in reality I was unprepared for the job. I learned quickly, though, how to cook on an institutional level, order food in mass quantities, manage personnel and learn about special diets. I filled in on every level, and took up the slack when employees were absent.

Cooking was the most demanding task in the department. Not only was it physically difficult, but it required a keen sense of timing. I struggled to lift hot, heavy pans from the ovens to the serving line. I used my body, mostly my hip, to act as another arm on which to rest the bulky pans. I used a cart, whenever I could, to transport food and asked for help when I couldn't manage by myself. I learned to be a fair grill cook and could keep up even during the busiest lunch time. I pushed awkward food carts to the patient floors, made individual and bulk salads, worked the tray line, racked dishes and served hot food in the cafeteria. Dealing with the staff, though, took more energy than I'd bargained for.

The older ladies on the staff resented me. They could tell that I was just learning the job, and they didn't appreciate my laid-back management style. The long, tedious hours became too much for me. The stress caused me to become physically ill. On top of that, I learned that the entire hospital was being moved across the street to a new facility. For the first time in my life I had to acknowledge that I was not Superwoman and could not continue to work a demanding, full-time job, go to college and manage my new household without damaging my health. Something had to go. I needed to simplify my life before I lost everything.

I had changed my college major more than once and was still undecided about which field of study to pursue. I had already decided, after working at the art house, that graphic art was not for me, but food service management still sounded exciting, and I needed to explore this area. So, for the time being, I postponed college in order to keep working in the food service field.

While working at the hospital, I had ordered institutional food products from Certified Grocers, a Los Angeles-based company with many advantages. Getting on with Certified looked promising; I was next in line for a position there as an inside-outside sales representative in institutional food sales. I resigned from the hospital and performed various in-between jobs until a position became available.

One of those jobs was as a quality control technician at a local snack-food producer. My responsibilities included performing a battery of tests at regular intervals on snack food items, which included potato, corn and tortilla chips. I was one of three "white" girls who worked the swing shift; the others were Mexican, some with questionable green cards. It didn't matter if they were white or Mexican to me, but the girls who worked in the factory were rugged types. There were often confrontations between the women, so the supervisor would separate the troublemakers between the two, expansive, chip-producing rooms. I often felt as if I were an outsider because I didn't speak Spanish. I felt fortunate to be in the quiet surroundings of the lab, insulated from the chip rooms. The factory environment was so loud that any time spent around the chip bagging machinery, which used compressed air for part of the process, left my ears ringing.

There was some concern by my immediate supervisor that I might have problems operating some of the testing equipment. Within a short time, though, I managed to keep up with the grueling amount of testing required during each hour for each product produced. There were salt tests to check the percentage of salt applied to the potato chips. Oil content evaluations on potato and tortilla chips. Water analysis on the masa, which was used to make tortilla chips and strips.

One evening, while performing routine tests, my concentration was suddenly broken by a commotion outside the lab. The shift supervisor, speaking rapidly in Spanish, was barking orders to other workers. Then he entered the lab and told me, in English, "Exit the building — *Now!*"

Without any further explanation from him, I walked out of the lab and into the room containing the potato fryer. To my horror I saw the fryer engulfed in bonfire-size flames. The intense fire reached all the way to the 25-foot-high ceiling. Thick, black, choking smoke filled the block-size potato-chip room. Terrified workers were attempting to escape the burning building, scattering like ants. Alarmed, I ran back inside my lab, telephoned the fire department, then joined others outside the partially incinerated factory.

The fire burned for 12 hours. The next day at work I was told that the bottom of the potato chip fryer had weakened and cracked. This allowed the hot grease to seep into the firebox below, which caused the entire vat of palm kernel oil to explode into flames. It amazed me to see how poorly my co-workers reacted to the menacing fire.

It was shortly after the life-threatening, snack-food-producer ordeal that I landed the job I wanted at Certified Grocers. The position was uncomplicated and satisfying. The only laborious part was fighting the freeway traffic from my home in Orange to the job in Los Angeles. But with my better salary I was able to sell my old frame house and buy a new townhome in Anaheim.

Chapter 3
Seeing Rudolf Gonzales, M.D.

At the time I was working for Certified Grocers as a sales representative, I decided to talk to the physician who had amputated my arm when I was three. I learned that he was still working in Gardena after 20 years, so I called and made an appointment to see him. I was curious about the amputation and wanted to hear his medical version of the events.

When I arrived at his office, I overheard him shouting at his secretary. I was unnerved and inquisitive. Later he revealed his conversation; he had not wanted to see me, fearing he'd be sued for malpractice. I assured him that my intentions were honest and that I wanted to see him for personal reasons. He started by saying he remembered the events vividly; he was a young physician, the accident was traumatic, not only for me, but for him. After being treated initially at a separate emergency room I was later transferred to the hospital and taken immediately into surgery.

"It was there," he said, "in the operating room, I saw you for the first time. I tried unsuccessfully to re-attach your arm, realizing there were delicate nerves missing."

He went on to explain that technology during the '50s,

After the amputation, 1958, with Grampa Cecil.

not being what it is now, left him with no choice but to amputate my arm in order to save my life.

I could tell he was a compassionate man. He knew what lifelong effect the amputation would have on me. He had agonized over his decision to try to save both my arm and my life. He added one further comment, "There has not been a year pass since the surgery that I haven't thought of you." He continued by saying, "I often wondered how you were doing, and if you had a full, productive life."

After I left his office I was numb. I couldn't stop thinking about our conversation. I never before understood that I was near death or that he had even attempted to re-attach my arm. Hearing these facts from him seemed less painful than from my parents and far more objective. The visit to Dr. Gonzales filled in gaps and satisfied my curiosity about the traumatic accident.

Chapter 4
Liquid Quarter Mile

W hile I was living in my new town home in Anaheim, I spent many weekends with my brother
and friends going to Parker, Arizona, to the boat
drags. Throughout the spring, summer and fall months,
several drag boat associations held races for willing partici-
pants. The drags were held at a number of rivers and lakes
which were set up with an official quarter-mile drag strip
complete with lights and markers, nicknamed the "Liquid
Quarter Mile." My brother Brian had an 18-foot, competition
flat-bottom boat with a 460-cubic-inch, injected, aluminum
engine which was mounted directly behind the driver. This
was a single-seat, very expensive, high-performance boat
intended for nothing more than running the quarter mile.

For three years we went to races in Arizona and California. It was fun and exciting because it was so dangerous. It
tempted the daring in both of us. For years, I watched Brian
race and helped work on the boat. Then he told me about
a powder puff race at Parker and asked if I wanted to enter
and drive the boat myself.

At first I said, "Brian, I don't want to be responsible for
a machine that cost you in excess of thirty-five thousand

dollars."

Brian replied encouragingly, "Try it!"

Never having driven a boat of this type, I needed practice, so Brian and I went out on the Colorado River for instruction. I sat in the driver's seat while he carefully knelt on the bottom deck of the boat, next to the five-gallon aluminum fuel tank. He explained the boat's particular operating characteristics and told me about the pedals on the floor — the one to the right was the gas pedal and to the left another pedal which consisted of two sections. The "Up and Down" pedal operated the boat's cavitation plate, located on the lower part of the stern. At the beginning of the quarter-mile run I would use the down pedal; after full power was added and the boat was "set" in the water, I would release the down pedal and depress the up pedal. The idea was to keep the boat straight with the down pedal which allowed the driver to maintain control after the initial burst of power. After the boat was "set" or sucked down into the water, using the up pedal would free or lift the boat up slightly for greater speed. Previous quarter-mile runs Brian had made in the boat were about eight seconds of elapsed time, at a top speed of 120 miles per hour. Everything happened quite rapidly. We spent about two hours on the river while I attempted to drive the boat. I was not sure, after such a poor practice run, if I would start the race, much less finish. After all, I'd never done it before.

The next morning dawned clear and still. The river was unusually smooth, reflecting the towering red rocks and scrubby brush growing on the opposite bank. Perfect for racing. There were only a handful of female competitors and we each took single runs down the race course. Brian helped me "suit up" for the race. I wore special ballistic pants, a full face helmet, and a life jacket that contained a small parachute. The idea behind the "chute" jacket, though it didn't work in all accident situations, was to keep the driver upright for a vertical landing in the water in case the boat crashed. The ballistic pants, made of bulletproof-type nylon, were worn to protect the stomach and groin area in case the boat splintered apart after a forceful impact with the water.

After I was seated, two additional lines were connected from the life jacket, one to the engine block for the chute jacket release and the other to an engine kill switch. If for some reason I was tossed out of the boat, the chute would be released and the engine would stop. The equipment was cumbersome and did not allow for freedom of movement, but, in the best interest of safety, was worn by every driver.

"Ladies, launch your boats!" was called by the announcer. "It's time to get your bottoms wet!"

As I was launched, a friend held the boat and me in the water, near the shore, until it was time to "Fire and Go." This meant to fire up the engine and get to the starting line. Finally, after anxiously waiting for other boats to make their runs, it was my turn. I started the boat, drove slightly down river and made a loop back toward the start line. Ahead was the "Christmas Tree," a floating tree of yellow, green and red lights which was used to begin each race. The yellow lights on the tree were flashing – this meant to slow the running start down slightly. I backed off the throttle somewhat but continued. I saw the green light and mashed the gas pedal to the floor. There was a tremendous thrust forward, and everything seemed to happen at once. I could hear only the

*The competition flatbottom boat Sheri drove to victory on
the Colorado River, near Parker, Arizona.*

powerful roar of the engine behind me, and I could see a blur
of water extending ahead. The boat was vibrating wildly. But
what rapid acceleration! I was hooked on the feeling —
speed!

The sensation was completely unparalleled by anything
I'd ever felt before. No carnival ride or roller coaster could
have prepared me for the tremendous acceleration forward.
In seconds, the finish line was behind me. I shut down the
engine and let the boat glide to a stop.

After the ladies' competition was over I returned to the
launch area. Brian told me I had a fantastic run. We hugged
each other while I fought back tears of joy, relief and success.
Then I found I had won the race with a speed of 92 miles per
hour and an elapsed time of 10.23 seconds. I couldn't believe
it! I hadn't even come close to the boat's top speed when
Brian drove it, but I still won.

That night at the awards presentation I claimed my prize,
a large, gold trophy with the inscription, "First Place." I

couldn't have been more overjoyed, or proud, of what I had accomplished. So much for the skeptics who didn't think I'd be able to hold on to the steering wheel with one arm, due to the force from the powerful engine, much less win the race!

Chapter 5
Finally Free?

By now, my life had taken on an obvious pattern. Just as soon as I had circumstances under control, had challenged myself with a new goal and met it, I was on to the next.

Driving to Los Angeles soon became an annoyance, and so I landed another job, managing food service facilities, at an exclusive racquetball/health club closer to home. My duties included formulating menus, hiring and training the staff, and ordering food and equipment. There were fringe benefits of club usage which made working there fun, and I learned to play racquetball from the on-staff pro. Since my balance was fairly good, and I had more than adequate eye/hand coordination, I found the game simple to understand, exciting and competitive – certainly not a two-handed game!

Life stayed busy with work, a roommate, a new house-cleaning business with a friend, and catering on weekends with an outside firm. As if this wasn't enough, I bought a horse. Since I'd been a child, I had wanted one of my own to ride, care for and love. It was a dream come true. This new friend, an 11-year-old grade mare, had a few poor habits. But, basically, she was very patient with me. I bought a saddle, necessary tack pieces, and spent what free time I had during evenings and weekends caring for her.

Saddling her was a strenuous task. My left arm was strong, but not strong enough to lift a 40-pound saddle over my head. I found it was easier if I positioned the mare close to a tack box I could stand on, with saddle in hand, and lift the saddle onto her back. Cinching was easy, and I rode with a hackamore, thus omitting the hassle of placing a bit in her mouth. I rode with a western saddle which allowed me to better develop my balance. I thought I'd try an English saddle later but never did.

I cared for the horse adequately, even though some aspects of grooming were not easy. For example, it took me a long time to pick up each of her feet and clean the inside of her hooves. I was persistent, however, and enjoyed owning her.

Work at the racquetball club, after more than a year, was waning. I was growing tired of living in an area that was becoming increasingly overcrowded, polluted and crime-ridden. I was also suffering from wanderlust. I knew there were places with cleaner air and fewer people, so I started looking for a food service management job that would allow me to travel, work in a variety of settings and meet new people from different cultures and backgrounds. Saga Food Service was such an organization.

Saga Food Service offered contract food service management to a variety of institutions, business and industry accounts, and to health care, college and school facilities.

I was hoping to work in Saga's Northern California region; instead, I was offered a position in Spokane, Washington, as a food service manager trainee for the Northwest

Division, based at Gonzaga University. I gladly accepted this assignment in the Pacific Northwest, leased my townhouse, donated my horse to a handicapped riding group and gave notice to the racquetball club, my roommate, friends, business partner and family that I was venturing north. During this transition I visited Spokane, found a place to live and returned to California to meet the movers. Now, life was really beginning...

I found Spokane, Washington, to be one of the most gorgeous places I'd ever seen. But it was, in many ways, different from Southern California. It was surrounded by areas of pine trees, lakes and vast wheat fields. I moved into a modest, secluded mobile home nestled in the pine trees seven miles south of town. It was in a spacious, quiet mobile home park, and I did have neighbors close by to help me get settled. I instantly knew I'd made the correct choice moving to the Pacific Northwest. The people I met in the workplace and in Spokane, generally, were pleasant, and life proceeded at a more relaxed pace than I'd been used to in Southern California.

The first six months I spent there, however, was as a hermit. I spent hours after work writing letters to family and friends at home in California, sewing and enjoying the outdoors. It was a special time for me because I felt completely self-reliant. I had to brave new experiences without the help of my parents or friends. The frigid winter weather was a new factor. Until then, I had never driven in snow, seen "black ice" or felt sub-zero temperatures.

My new job went favorably at first, but it wasn't uncomplicated, and upon returning home in the evenings, there was no one to share the day's events with. To compound my misery, I was not seeing eye-to-eye with Terry, my boss, who was in charge of my training. He seemed resentful of me, and I often thought he felt threatened because I was a capable, intelligent woman. As hard as I tried to get on his wave length, it seemed I couldn't please him. There was something wrong somewhere. His management style was, in my opinion, not a positive motivator for me or other staff members. If he became upset, for example, about a food item not being prepared to his exact standard, he might have a temper tantrum in the middle of the kitchen, but out of view of the paying customers. This completely disrupted the work flow, errors were made and employees made more mistakes, sometimes inadvertently injuring themselves.

Since I was a trainee, I was allowed to travel to various units of the Saga system to work and gain experience. This permitted me to keep my distance from Terry and, at the same time, learn about the special operating procedures at each facility. I worked as an assistant in business and industry accounts, at a retirement home for Catholic sisters, and in the four units which furnished college food service at Gonzaga University. I was two weeks at one account, a month at another and later relieved managers who left for vacation.

I valued all the moving around. My three-week assignment in Kalamazoo, Michigan, for company management school was especially absorbing. I got to travel at someone else's expense, see the country and experience diverse ways of living. Kalamazoo was my first exposure to the Midwest, or at least what I thought of as the Midwest. I started there in December — cold, snow and three weeks of gray skies.

The school housed us three and four to an apartment.

One of my roommates was from New York, the other from Boise, Idaho. Paula, from New York, was of Greek descent, and I found her language and background fascinating. Cathy, from Boise, was more of a down-home girl. A registered dietitian, she was creative, earthy and well-educated. The three of us sat up for hours each night after class talking about our lives and the food business.

We found the schedule at Saga School punishing. Days were long, often starting at 5:30 in the morning and not ending until well past seven at night. Then there was homework. During our stay, we cooked, planned menus, visited other Saga accounts for meals and worked on several other facets of food service management, including accounting and employee relations. At no time was any mention made of my arm, or rather the lack of it. I appreciated the fair treatment and thought well of the company for that reason.

At the end of the nearly month-long stint, there was an evaluation process. During the evaluation we learned how successful we might be in the food business with Saga, how we had done in school and what our account assignment would be, once we returned to our home base. Most everyone in class received assignments but me. I was worried. I wanted so much to return to a food service director position at an account other than Gonzaga, but instead – much to my dismay – I returned to my original college account.

I continued to work as a trainee until the following spring, when I was told by Terry and Sid, Terry's boss and district manager, that I would be operating the Cog dining hall facility at Gonzaga. Sam, the existing manager, would be transferred to a larger account. My heart sank. How was I going to cope with Terry any longer? How was I ever going to perform my duties well enough to satisfy him? Then, there was the account itself — huge by industry standards, understaffed, and with a less-than-adequate kitchen and serving facility.

During the summer months I worked at the dining hall mostly by myself, cleaning the kitchen and managing other dining halls while their managers went on vacation. I worked with my full-time staff of employees, five student managers and a student crew, providing food service for weekly conferences. I moved from the mobile home park to a duplex apartment near campus. I barely got settled between conferences.

One conference was a group of priests from all parts of the Pacific Northwest, another was a conference for 1,500 Indians. The Indians, from a variety of tribes located as far east as Nebraska, brought their tepees, which they pitched on the grounds outside the dining hall. In addition to the food we provided, they had large, open pit fires where they arranged large filets of fresh, pink salmon that had been woven onto sticks, then stuck in the ground around the fire pit to cook.

As August approached, my staff and I were preparing ourselves for the return of the students. Counts were finally in: my dining hall would feed 766 students, 20 meals each week. Additionally, I was responsible for catered sit-down meals for as many as 400 people or as few as three, and for snack bar operations in the lower Cog.

Constant planning was necessary to manage the dining hall operation — more than I had envisioned. I was responsible for all meals, which included those served on my days off. I was beginning to feel used. Terry was never pleased with the results of my operation, unless the bottom line contributed to his bonus. He insisted that I tightly manage my "piece of business."

A typical day in the dining hall started right after breakfast. I placed food orders, handled personnel shortages and daily equipment failure, got set up for lunch, checked on whatever catered meal was also being served — a lunch for the college president, for example — made myself visible and communicated with students at lunchtime. I went on to handle accounting, meal planning, staff meetings and a conference with Terry. Then I prepared for dinner, during which I again had to make myself visible to students in order to prevent food fights or other disruptions in the dining hall. Often there was an event to be catered in the evening. I never sat down to eat a meal and soon lost 30 pounds.

I dealt with the stress the best I could, but it was a losing battle. I found myself, during the meager spare time I had, turning to male companionship and plenty of alcohol consumption. I was ignorant of the fact that various managers before me had become alcoholics as a result of the tremendous pressure and long hours. One previous manager kept a small bottle of Scotch in his desk drawer and turned to it during moments of crisis at the dining hall. This "moment of crisis" might be precipitated by the accidental burning of a food item for a catered event or the discovery that a specific canned goods item had been used up and needed to be replaced at once. Progress came to a halt in the kitchen until a substitution was available.

I was gradually drinking more and more to drown and chemically overcome the perpetual physical and emotional strain of the hectic dining hall conditions. One workday morning about 11 o'clock, I realized I was craving a beer. I could taste it. I could think of nothing else. That's when I knew I had to stop. I reflected at that moment on a relative who had spent a lifetime as a heavy drinker and who had often abused other drugs. I always resented his unpredictable behavior in a social situation and his unyielding addictions. For that reason I knew I needed to find an alternative for the insidious alcohol that had become an obscene part of my life.

Chapter 6
Solo Flight

I'd lived in Spokane for nearly a year when, on one bar-hopping Saturday night, I met a man who would forever change my life. As my girlfriend and I sat drinking and looking for Mr. Right, I turned to greet the man sitting next to me. He told me his name was Al Anderson. My first impression was not all that favorable, though he did look striking in his brown leather flight jacket. He was obviously drunk. As we began to talk, he told me he was a pilot and lived near Moses Lake, Washington, in Warden, a quaint farming town. He managed a farm and grain warehouse there, was divorced and had two sons who lived with him. As the evening progressed, Al's friend Keith and my girl-friend went on to another bar. I had to get home because Sunday brunch at the college came early, and, since Al was ready to leave, I dropped him off at his hotel nearby. When I told him good-night he said, sheepishly, "Wouldn't you like to have my phone number?" I felt sorry for him and agreed to exchange phone numbers.

In a day or two I heard from him. This time he was sober. He asked if I'd like to accompany him to Priest Lake, in northern Idaho, for snowmobiling. It would be an overnight trip, and for a moment I was stunned. I didn't know this man, but my gut feeling said, "trust him." So I decided to go and prepared to enjoy the new snow cover and my first snowmobiling adventure.

We rode tandem on the snowmobile, Al at the controls and me clinging tightly, like a frightened monkey, to his backside. I would like to have driven, but the machine had controls like a motorcycle — clutch on one side of the handlebars and throttle on the other — definitely a two-handed arrangement. Between snowmobiling sessions we visited the local tavern at the lodge for a robust red beer, a combination of beer and tomato juice.

Al turned out to be delightful and entertaining. I enjoyed his outgoing style and willingness to try new adventures. He told me more about his life in Warden and his troubles at the grain warehouse. He felt that the farm and the warehouse were being mismanaged and that the board of directors wasn't giving him the control he needed to run both at a profit. It sounded like a baffling situation for him. As it turned out, the snowmobiling trip was a tension reliever for both of us.

After returning home, I heard from Al again, this time inviting me to visit him at his farm in Warden. I accepted. I was to find out that his life was unlike anything I knew or expected. After I arrived, Al took me for a tour of the farm. He lived in a double-wide mobile home with an indoor recreational facility behind it, which he had built with his boys in mind. Inside the building was a combination racquetball/basketball court, garage, office and hot tub. Outside was a round dirt track, complete with sand buggy. Beyond this was an area where his boys raised sheep as a 4-H project.

Farther down the hill stood a huge metal structure that housed various kinds of farm equipment. Outside the steel building were the cattle pens and acre after acre of beef cattle.

That afternoon, Al offered to show me the grain warehouse where local farmers purchased feed, fertilizer and seed. We also went for a tour of Warden and the surrounding area. During our sight-seeing trip Al told me about how he became a pilot. I told him I'd wanted to fly since I was a child but never had the opportunity. He said, "Well, let's see if you can fly!"

Shortly, we arrived at Warden's airport, a 3,300-foot, paved landing strip. We pulled up next to a diminutive, high-wing, two-place airplane, and Al checked its airframe, fuel and oil. "We're ready," he said. "Hop in!"

I didn't ask, "Whose plane IS this?" or, "It's so little — is it safe?" Again, an instinctive trust of Al and my sense of adventure overcame any negative feelings I might have had.

After belting us in, Al explained what the controls did and how they affected flight. I'd work the steering wheel and foot pedals, which I later found out were the yoke and rudder control. He would work the throttle. Both sides of the aircraft panel had full controls, yoke and rudder pedals, which made me feel safer. I sat in the right seat because Al felt the left seat might be troublesome if at any time I wanted to reach the throttle.

He taxied to the end of the runway, positioned the small plane into the wind, added full power and began our takeoff roll. At what seemed a slow speed to me, and without much control input from Al, I noticed the ground starting to fall away, and we were flying!

I watched all the dials on the dashboard (which I later found out was called the instrument panel) change as we slowly climbed. Al leveled off and gave me the controls. I tried some gentle turns, climbs and descents. It took less movement of the controls than I thought it would.

After what seemed like only five minutes to me – but really more like half an hour – we returned to the airport. I remember seeing a set of lights alongside the runway. Al had explained that their purpose was to help the pilot keep the correct height in relationship to the horizontal distance from the approach end of the runway, and now he was yelling at me to keep the top light red, the bottom one white. I was having a tough time staying in control. One minute the lights were white-white, the next red-red. Finally, much to my relief, he took command and brought us to a safe, smooth landing.

The entire ordeal was more than I could handle, and Al's lack of patience made it worse. After that flight with him, I wasn't sure I wanted to learn to fly.

Years earlier, when I was a teenager, I wanted to learn to fly. I would drive my Camaro up to Fullerton Airport, watch aircraft do touch 'n' goes and pump avgas into my car, all the time pretending it was a flying machine. At that time I inquired about flying and was told that, in order to operate the airplane, I would have to have one hand on the yoke, the other on the throttle. These same thoughts haunted me again as I reconsidered flying. Maybe flying really was a two-handed activity. Maybe it would be dangerous or impossible to attempt lessons.

As Al and I talked about it, though, he said he thought I could fly if I wanted to. I think he realized that I was motivated by a lifelong desire and probably had the coordination to learn, but there were many questions that I needed answered. We would talk to several people about my desire to fly — first, someone at the Federal Aviation Administration, and second, someone who could teach me the skills necessary to become a private pilot. Al suggested that, during one of his regular visits to Spokane, we could see an instructor at Felts Field Aviation located in the Spokane Valley, east of downtown Spokane.

We met with Dave, the chief pilot at the school. Al did most of the talking, but I didn't miss any of the details. He told Dave that he knew they had an excellent reputation for flight training and he wanted the best for me. Dave explained that having a student like me, with only one arm, would be a new situation for them. Finally Dave turned to me and said in a conceding voice, "Our instructors will try to teach you to fly, but the school will make no guarantees that you can become a private pilot." He suggested that I speak to the FAA and see what their feelings were about my impairment.

So I went, alone this time, to meet with a general aviation safety inspector at the local Flight Standards District Office, conveniently located on the field at Felts. I told the inspector about my desire to fly and asked if having one arm would keep me from being a private pilot. His answer was, "Go Fly!"

As I walked away, I remember thinking how long it had been since the subject of my having one arm was so thoroughly discussed. For several years I'd not given it much thought, had gone on with my life as if I were whole. So far, this experience had brought me back to reality, and there was more of the same to come.

I started my flight training twice a week during my afternoon and sole day off from Gonzaga in January, 1983. The aircraft for training purposes was a Cessna 172 (four-place aircraft) and initial flights were with Jim Bening, the chief flight instructor at Felts Field Aviation.

After the first lesson, which consisted of aircraft/environment familiarization and use of controls, Jim said I needed some sort of device to keep the aircraft stable while I took my hand off the yoke and reached for the throttle or elevator trim tab. He worked with me discreetly, one-on-one, to find out what I needed to help me through my flight training. He was honest, knowledgeable, genuinely interested, and extremely helpful, which I sincerely appreciated. This was an intense time for me because I wanted so much to become a pilot, yet I was overly sensitive to my situation. I didn't really know yet if flying would be an option for me. After two lessons it was even more apparent that I would need an artificial arm, so lessons were postponed until after I saw a prosthetics designer.

I met with two designers, explained my needs and budget, and a week later they presented me with a prosthetic "device." It had two pieces – the first was an 18-inch piece of plastic sprinkler pipe attached to a used, artificial right hand; the second was a curved piece of thick leather with a female connector protruding from its middle, where the pipe could be attached. A long section of flat-braided, one-inch-wide fabric was attached to the end of the leather piece and went under what remained of my right arm, across my back in a figure-eight fashion, over then under my left arm, then back to the other end of the leather piece. The braid was then fed through another bracket, folded over itself toward the back and held in place with a wide Velcro™ fastener. I first put on the figure-eight harness and then screwed the hand/pipe into the shoulder piece.

The cost to me for this innovative contraption was a modest $35.00. The well-worn hand slid snugly over the top of the open yoke in the aircraft and was just what I needed to control pitch (up and down) movement of the aircraft.

I resumed flight lessons at once and was becoming attached to Jim because of his patience, assistance and understanding. I was disturbed when he told me he was turning me over to Steve Rezin, a new instructor. At first, I was reluctant to change, and I wondered if he'd be as positive and helpful as Jim had been. Later on, Steve did admit that, in the beginning, he didn't think I could learn to fly using one hand, but that he soon realized I was so motivated and enthusiastic that there was no way I would stop. I *would* find a way.

Flying became my escape and slowly took the place of alcohol in my life. I realized that alcohol had been an evil reprieve for me – a way to relax and forget about the unrelenting grind of a typical day at the dining hall. Alcohol was treacherous. I didn't like the taste but thirsted for how I felt as a result. The worries of the job at Saga had seemed overwhelming without it. Now flying had replaced alcohol as a new drug – a new addiction, but a much healthier one. At least I thought so at the time.

I adored going to the airport – I was stimulated by both the environment and the comradeship with the other pilots, who seemed to be an exhilarating, brazen group. Also, there were few women interested in flying, which made the odds all the better for me to find male companionship.

During the first 21 hours of flight lessons, and before I soloed, I had to obtain a Third-Class Medical Certificate. I visited an Federal Aviation Administration approved medical examiner, and after I passed all the required tests, the doctor, a seasoned aviator, issued me the student pilot medical certificate. But this was not done without his words of wisdom — all negative. He started to lecture me as I sat semi-clothed on the examining table.

"I am an experienced pilot," he boasted. "I don't know *how* you are going to manage any aircraft under normal and simulated emergency procedures." His face expressed growing skepticism, like a festering storm cloud. "I don't know how you are going to make it through the training it would take to get a private pilot's license," he said.

Damn, I thought, why was he so pessimistic? It was hardly what I expected from a member of the medical profession, much less a fellow pilot. But I wasn't going to be discouraged.

Despite Steve's restrained misgivings, my flying progressed to the point where I was about to solo. I didn't know at that time that if I botched my solo flight — had an accident for example — Steve's flight instructor certificate and career might be in jeopardy. But he obviously felt that I handled the aircraft properly and met specific written and practical completion standards needed to solo.

Somehow the local newspaper caught wind of my first solo attempt, and a reporter met me at the airport the day I was to solo. She asked many questions, and the photographer with her wanted to take pictures of me with my instructor on board the aircraft. They were especially interested in my prosthetic device, which I had appropriately

Using "Handy" on a dual instructional flight with Steve Rezin.

named, "Handy." I wanted to be an inspiration to others, so I agreed to photos and a story, but in the back of my mind I wondered if they secretly wished they could cover doom and gloom. Did they want to be first on the scene of an airplane crash with a one-armed pilot at the controls?

They watched as my instructor and I made three takeoff and landing efforts in the traffic pattern. Then we returned to the school. I kept the aircraft engine running while Steve signed my medical certificate for solo flight, then departed the airplane. "Do three touch 'n' goes, then return to the school," he said calmly.

I closed the left door and locked it, obtained a clearance from the tower controller, slowly taxied to the approach end of the runway, obtained an additional clearance and took off without hesitation. I felt confident, well prepared and ready to fly by myself. I talked out loud to myself during the first two takeoffs and landings. It was as if Steve were at my side, speaking to me. Instead of doing three takeoffs and landings, I went against Steve's orders and did five. The thrill of soloing was that invigorating. I later realized his reasons for me to do only three; afterward, I was absolutely exhausted.

The following day, in the morning edition of the *Spokes-man Review*, second section, was an entire front page dedicated to my solo flight at Felts Field. It was an impressive story, well written with several large photographs of me, Steve and the solo aircraft. This story was sent out over the Associated Press wire with one of the photos.

Within a week's time I received a telephone call from a reporter in Florida representing the *Weekly World News*. During our conversation, she said, "The paper thought the AP story was inspirational." She continued in a melodious inflection, "With your permission, Sheri, I would like a telephone interview, including a personal account of your solo, since we often print such triumphant stories."

I agreed to her request, thinking at the time that if I positively touched the life of *one* person with my story, I had made the correct decision to grant the interview.

The reporter and I talked for nearly a half an hour, and she said she would send me a tear sheet from the paper so I could see the printed results. Less than a month later, the tear sheet from the paper arrived.

To my embarrassment, I found the article named me as a cripple and printed other lies. I felt exploited, manipulated, used and justifiably angry.

I never indicated to the reporter I was a cripple, disabled or handicapped. Why did they write such untruths about me? Why did they publicly degrade me?

After some research, I learned the paper was a weekly gossip magazine sold at grocery store checkout counters. A common, malicious, dirty rag that sensationalized the smallest innocent story. It was the kind of paper that intends to grab the attention of curious shoppers waiting in line to check out. Disgusted and humiliated, I never shared the article with anyone. I wanted so much for it to be helpful; instead it only became unprofessional media exploitation. I hated to think that from such an optimistic aviation story could come a twisted, misleading lie from the editors of the *Weekly World News.*

After the first solo flight, there was more dual with Steve and more solo time before we started our cross-country segment. During one of these solo flights and after flying north of the airport to practice specific maneuvers, I realized that clouds were rapidly surrounding my aircraft on three sides. I knew better than to fly near or in them, and promptly headed away and back toward the airport. Clouds were directly over the airport, too, and in my flight path, so I had to change my course and head farther east. At the same time, it was necessary to descend to stay under the encroaching overcast. I turned west toward the field, but visibility was getting worse. I descended again, called the control tower at Felts and requested a landing clearance. After giving me clearance, the controller told me the current conditions at the field. "Cessna 64875, the ceiling is 800 overcast, one mile visibility, in heavy rain," he advised.

I called the tower back and said in a shaky voice, "I am having difficulty finding the field."

After seeing my aircraft on the radar screen, the tower controller assured me that I was on the proper heading. I continued westward, thinking I had to go home. After all, I had never landed at any other airport during a solo flight. As I flew closer to the field, the rain started out gentle, then it grew so intense that I couldn't see out the windscreen. It was hitting the aircraft so violently that it sounded like millions of ball bearings.

This is it, I thought. *I'm going to die.*

I methodically evaluated my options: I could turn around and look for improved weather or continue. At that moment I realized I was in control of my own destiny. I was still flying the airplane. Controls and engine were still operational, so I decided to continue to Felts Field. I could barely make out the VASI lights (red over white) through the rain-drenched windscreen as I approached the end of Runway 21 from the east. With nearly no forward vision and the noisy distraction of the heavy rain on the airframe, I collected all my concentration and made one of the best landings ever.

After taxiing to the school and telling Steve about my trial, he said, "Come out to the airport this afternoon and solo again." As a flight instructor, he knew that a positive experience must follow a negative one or the school risks losing a student. I took his advice and flew that afternoon again, by myself, which renewed my confidence.

Chapter 7

Goodbye Spokane

As my flight training progressed, I had a variety of other experiences which added up to an exhilarating learning process. The pilots at Felts knew I was absorbed in every aspect of aviation and so offered to expose me to as much information and opportunity as I had time for. In the meantime, I was making new friends and keeping Al updated on my progress. I had taken my training semi-seriously; it had been challenging, but I'd succeeded, though at that point I never thought I'd continue on to be a professional pilot.

I had started flight training in January 1983. It was now July, and I met with Del Randall from the FAA for my checkride, which would also satisfy demonstrated ability requirements for my third-class medical certificate. We started off with an extensive oral exam, for which I had been well prepared by Jim Bening. After I passed the oral exam, Del carefully watched me preflight the Cessna 172, making sure I could jump up on the step and visually check the fuel.

One of the FAA's criteria for passing the checkride with impaired pilots is that the pilot must be able to meet all completion standards without assistance. This included every aspect, from preflight through and including post-flight procedures. I was neither nervous, shy nor embarrassed as I twisted on "Handy" and put the prosthesis in place over the top portion of the yoke. I did ask Del if there might be a way to have an unrestricted medical certificate; I did not want to have to wear Handy forever. He thought there might be a way, but didn't commit himself at that point.

I started the aircraft, obtained a clearance and taxied out to the run-up area, being careful to follow the detailed checklist every step of the way. We headed outbound from Felts to the west and south of downtown Spokane. He quickly noticed that I was nether apprehensive nor lacking in confidence. I performed the maneuvers as he asked and to better-than-standard, including emergency procedures.

Finally, he directed me to fly to Deer Park, an uncontrolled field north of Spokane. Once there, he took control of the aircraft and asked me to take off "my arm." He laughed out loud as I slowly untwisted Handy and put it under my seat.

"I have told women to take off other things but never an arm!" he said. He went on to tell me that if I indeed wanted an unrestricted certificate, he would need to see several touch 'n' goes in the pattern, without the use of Handy. These I managed with ease, and after Del made a few landings, we returned to Felts Field.

As we taxied back to the FAA building, he told me I did a fine job. After I shut the aircraft down, he said, "I think we'll make you an FAA-certified private pilot!"

As I exited the airplane, Jim Bening rushed to greet me with a big hug. "I knew you could do it!" he said, proudly.

I felt elated, astounded. My heart was beating wildly with

excitement. I had done what everyone thought would be impossible! And I had done it with a minimum of mental, physical and emotional hardship. I say not much hardship, but there were factors involved that I never thought might be an issue, such as having to get Handy made. But I realized that getting the private pilot rating was a turning point in my life. I was setting goals and achieving the seemingly unimaginable.

Granted, I was highly motivated by my love of flying and my enjoyment of life in three dimensions, but the secret was in being persistent. I was determined to get that private rating, despite any reservations the doctor or unacquainted pilots at Felts might have had and despite the fact that Terry, my boss at Gonzaga, had told me that if I could do it, obviously *he* could do it. What a no-confidence boost. What a jerk!

If I could fly, I could figure out how to do *anything* with one arm. It might take me longer, I might need to be more patient or clever, but *where there was a will there was a way.* I cannot emphasize this philosophy enough because many times throughout my life it has been true.

After the private rating, my motto was, "What's next?" I decided I would see just how far I could go in aviation. I started by getting checked out in bigger, faster and more complex aircraft. I carefully studied each new aircraft operating handbook so that I was well versed in each speed of operation, emergency procedure and aircraft system.

Eight days after getting my private rating, I was checked out in a Cessna 182, which was a six cylinder, 235-horsepower, variable-pitch-propeller, four-place, stable, excellent, cross-country traveling airplane.

First Dual in a Pitts Special with Keith Aneliff at Henly Aerodrome in northern Idaho, 1982.

Terry, back at the hash factory, was barely able to congratulate me on my latest achievement. But he didn't hesitate to ask me if I might fly him to his home in Malta, Montana, to see his ailing parents. He would pay at least half of the expenses, so I agreed to take him in the C-182.

I carefully planned the trip across the wide expanse of mountain ranges which exist east of Spokane and extend almost to Great Falls, Montana. From Great Falls, we would fly to Malta. The trip was eventful.

Mistake number one was leaving in the afternoon, late in summer, when the threat of thunderstorms was greatest. It was a sweltering afternoon and thermals and updrafts off the mountains caused a moderate amount of turbulence. Terry was conspicuously nervous, and there was nothing for him to hold on to inside the cockpit as the rough air buffeted us about.

Sheri preflighting a Cessna Turbo Centurion at Felts Field, December, 1983.

I attempted to calm him but to no avail. I did entertain the fleeting thought that this was one way to get back at him for all the times he had made me agitated in the dining hall.

Our landings at Great Falls and Malta were without incident, and the return trip was routine. I considered my first long-cross-country trip, especially over forbidding mountains and in a new aircraft, to be remarkably successful.

From September 1983 until February 1984, I continued to fly at Felts. I was checked out in a C-172 with retractable gear, a C-Turbo 210 and took a number of local and cross-country trips. During this time I also earned a single-engine seaplane rating, which, to this day, was the most enchanting rating I ever worked on. While flying a seaplane, I cherished the thrill of having a boat and an airplane combined in one craft.

Events at Gonzaga were getting worse. Terry was relentless. I had never seemed to please him completely before, but now he asked for even more than I thought he should. A transfer to another facility where I'd have more responsibility as food service director didn't seem to immediately be in the cards. Transfers did not typically come during the middle of the school year.

I loathed my job. The long, tedious hours became a more prolonged grind, and I decided I'd had enough of the Cog dining-hall routine, Gonzaga and, most of all, fatuous Terry. It was so bad that the flying was not enough of an escape, so I asked the company for a transfer to the health care division. The health care division management realized I had superior health care/institutional food service management skills, plus a glowing record with Saga. So, rather than risk losing me, they offered me a position.

My job was management reserve – traveling from facility to facility to fill in as needed and, at the same time, learn about each new operation. I was delighted about the opportunities; and, the health care division was growing at a much faster rate than the education division. I was finally away from Terry, and this relieved me from an enormous amount of stress.

I lived for a brief period of time in Lewiston, Idaho, and then Seattle, Washington. At each location, I checked out in a C-172. This not only kept me current as a pilot but gave me a complete aerial view of the local area. Finally I was assigned to Billings Deaconess Hospital in Billings, Montana, as a food service manager. I thought all along that Spokane was a great experience, so why wouldn't Billings be, too?

Chapter 8
Disaster and Darkness

W hen I approached Billings from the west, driving on Interstate 90, I was not impressed. I expected the city to be closer to the mountains and to have more trees, especially pines. But instead I saw the start of the high plains. The land looked dry, and rocky buttes with flat tops were scattered about. Billings was in a depression surrounded by these "rims," as the locals called them.

Through the area flowed the Yellowstone River. To the southwest were the Beartooth Mountains, to the southeast the Big Horn Mountains, to the west the Crazy Mountains and to the northwest the Snowy's. To the east, high plains reached all the way to the Black Hills of South Dakota.

Billings seemed small, after Spokane, and very isolated. The downtown area was about a fourth the size of Spokane's, and department stores were few, except for one fairly new mall on the west end of town. Though it was not what I'd anticipated, I decided to make the most of it. I immediately went to the new account, Billings Deaconess Hospital, to meet my new manager, Food Service Director Roger, and other members of the dietary staff. I set out the next morning to find a suitable apartment. After several days of looking, I decided on a conservative and economical attic apartment close to the hospital.

After getting settled at work and getting into a daily routine, I made a beeline for the airport. There I found an experienced flight instructor and started working toward additional ratings – instrument and commercial.

Though I spent long busy hours at work, it still wasn't as taxing as Gonzaga. I liked my supervisor, Roger; he didn't seem threatened by my independent nature. My job was basically to see that production standards were being met for the patient tray line, a small employee cafeteria, and the larger employee/visitor cafeteria across the street.

When not at work or flying, I was busy making new friends. I got involved once again with the 99's, as I had briefly in Spokane. The 99's is an international organization of female pilots who promote safety, education and general aviation. The gals in the 99's were stimulating, supportive and adventurous. We worked together to airmark airports with their names and sponsored pinch-hitting courses for pilots' spouses, so they might feel better about the cockpit environment. The 99's were a distinguished network to be part of.

During the spring of 1984, I went to Lewiston to the Montana Pilots' Association yearly meeting, where I received the Bill Mathews Award. I was recommended for this by Patty Mitchell, a 99's friend, who realized that I was trying to accomplish more in aviation than most pilots with two arms. The award was given to one individual each year for outstanding personal achievement in aviation, while overcoming special circumstances. I was honored to receive it and promised myself that I would live up to the association's expectations.

During this period, I met Anne Stevens, a fellow female pilot. She was living with a man who owned a C-172. Since we had access to it at a reduced rental rate, we went on several journeys together. Anne was more than assertive, and, in her quest for a professional pilot position, eventually managed to anger everyone in the local pilot community, including me. But we had many good experiences together before that happened. I was feeling quite cocky, myself – I had a respectable, well-paying, responsible position with Saga, enough money to fly and travel, and was making friends and enjoying what Billings and the surrounding area had to offer.

Billings, and Montana in general, was an informal place to live. There were few hassles and only one minor setback that I could think of related to state government. It became necessary for me to replace my driver's license, since I had a Washington State driver's license. In both California and Washington I had no restrictions to my driving privileges. I expected to go to the driver's licensing division, fill out the necessary forms, and be on my way with the Montana driver's license in hand.

I approached the clerk at the window of the license division, explained what I wanted and then waited. She looked at my Washington driver's license, started the paperwork, stopped, then with a doubting face, looked at me. I could see her eyes travel down my face, then stop at my empty right arm sleeve. Then, in an authoritative voice, she said, "You'll have to take a driver test in a manual-transmission-type car to prove to us you can operate it safely."

I was outraged. I released my fury replying, caustically, "I have had no prior restrictions, so why, then, because of the way my body looks, should you have decided a driving test is necessary?"

It seemed my energy was being wasted on the foolish woman. I had no choice, it seemed, if I wanted an unrestricted license. At the time, I was driving an automatic-transmission-type car, one of the few I've ever owned. Later that afternoon I borrowed Anne's stick-shift sports car, returned to the licensing division and took the driver's test. Although I never left second gear during the test, which convinced me it was a farce, I proved to the division I could drive the manual transmission. I received my unrestricted driver's license shortly thereafter.

Finally, and for the first time in my life, I had nearly everything I wanted — except a meaningful relationship. Finding "Mr. Right" was an ongoing goal. It was more difficult in Montana than it had been elsewhere to find sincere, nice-looking men with something favorable happening in their lives. Meanwhile, I had a new friend to pal around with. Julie Payne, from Idaho, was my assistant at the hospital, and since she was single, we enjoyed going to look at men and other sights afforded by the local hot spots.

One sunny afternoon in late May, since it was our afternoon off, I persuaded Julie to go with me to the airport to see if anything exciting was going on at the fixed-base operation where I'd been taking flight lessons. At Lynch Flying Service we struck up a conversation with Bob and Bill, two very congenial men, obviously on their way flying somewhere. After a while, they asked if we'd like to go with them to Recluse, Wyoming, where Bob was to visit his son, who worked on a ranch.

Without much thought, we jumped into Bob's C-210 (a high-performance, six-place, retractable-gear, single-engine aircraft). The pilots, Bob and I, rode up front, with non-pilots Julie and Bill in the back seat. Since I didn't know where Recluse was, I offered to get out the aeronautical charts and help with navigation. I pinpointed the exact place on the sectional map by means of a VOR (a navigational instrument) cross check and suggested to Bob that he intercept a specific radial from Sheridan VOR and track it until crossing a specific radial from Gillette VOR. "After crossing the radial from Gillette VOR," I said confidently, "we should be at or near Recluse."

Bob seemed confused about this procedure and stubbornly continued on. We began to get off course slightly, and Bob didn't seem to have his whole attention on flying. After circling the Recluse area, he found the unobtrusive grass strip, located beside a cow pasture, and landed.

Our stay in Recluse was brief. Bob saw his son, we went to the local store for something to drink and then back to the aircraft for our return to Billings. The weather was ideal, and though our fuel tank was less than full, we had plenty for the return flight.

Being a conscientious, low-time private pilot, I got out Bob's C-210 aircraft manual and calculated a takeoff distance of 1,950 feet. The grass strip was about 2,500 feet long and ran north to south. Though there were telephone wires at the far end of the strip, I knew we'd have plenty of room to clear them.

I finished my calculations and reported them to Bob, but he brushed them off as insignificant. Again I told him I knew

I wasn't pilot-in-command and didn't want to interfere, that I was only practicing.

Bob started the aircraft and, for some reason, taxied slightly west of the departure end of the strip to start the takeoff roll. Keeping the yoke in his lap, Bob abruptly added full power, and the aircraft yawed sharply to the left of his intended flight path. He kept his head inside the cockpit, eyes fixed on the airspeed indicator.

Though the nose was at a high angle, I could see we were drifting farther and farther away from the strip. Once or twice I said, "Bob, looks like you need more right rudder." Right rudder application controls the left-turning tendency caused by engine torque and other left-turning factors at high angles of attack, for example, on takeoff.

The takeoff roll seemed to take an eternity. We should be off by now, I thought. We were not on the grass runway but to the left of it. The ground was wet; there was standing water beneath us. The prop cut through the tall grass like a sharp sickle, and the ride became very rough. We were approaching a 12- to 14-foot berm of dirt near the edge of the cow pasture, and Bob still had his head inside the cockpit.

As the berm loomed larger I thought, *this guy is going to wreck his airplane!* I'm only a passenger. If he wants to wreck it, it's his business.

That turned out to be a disastrous mistake. Bob looked up, saw the approaching berm and, in a panic, horsed the aircraft off the ground. At 45 to 50 knots airspeed, the aircraft was not ready to fly. Air flowing over the wings at that slow speed was not enough to support the weight of the aircraft and let it fly. The drag from the tall grass, standing water and mushy pasture, at an angle west of the flight path, was too great to allow the necessary acceleration. The airplane flew briefly with a momentous hop.

As we approached the ground, Bob tried to flare so that the airplane could touch down on the main gear. Instead the tail forcefully struck the ground, causing the nose of the aircraft to pitch forward. With full power still applied, the nose gear struck a raised embankment of a pond to the left of the tall berm. We all tried to hold on to whatever we could inside the cockpit. Two or three more times the aircraft leaped into the air and nosed back to the ground, each time causing further damage.

Though I had my seat belt fastened securely about my pelvis, without the benefit of a shoulder harness, I felt my head smash violently into the instrument panel with each impact of the aircraft to the ground. Again and again, I felt like I was getting whacked in the forehead with a baseball bat at full swing. Then I lost consciousness.

Julie later told me the details of the airplane crash. The airplane finally came to rest at the far northwest corner of the pasture, its propeller and gear folded underneath, engine torn away from the firewall, wings collapsed. Avgas flowed profusely from each wing. Julie and Bill, unhurt but terribly shaken, pulled my limp body from the damaged aircraft and laid me down a short distance from the wreckage. Bob, still conscious but in shock, attempted to light several cigarettes and fortunately was stopped by his own son, who had been a witness.

Several local people heard the crash and came to help. The pungent smell of avgas filled the air. One man, Fred Oedekoven, and his son reached the scene within minutes.

Airplane crash in Recluse, Wyoming, 1984.

As I lay unconscious on the ground, the young boy excitedly pointed out to his dad that I was missing an arm – he thought, as a result of the crash. But, of course, there was no blood.

I don't know how long it was before I finally came to and saw both Bill and Julie kneeling over me. Everything appeared dark. Inside my head was mass confusion. I saw an aura similar to one I had seen at the start of a migraine stress headache. My forehead thumped with massive pain, and I could not talk.

Julie said softly, "Sheri, do you know we've been in an airplane crash?"

With all the effort I could muster, I said to Julie, "How's my face?"

"Okay," she said, trying not to laugh at my single-minded concern, "except for one place."

There was a bleeding hole about the size of a quarter on

the right side of my forehead near the hairline.

By then, someone arrived with a Suburban truck, and I was loaded into it with Bill, Julie and Bob, and sent to meet an ambulance from Gillette. While in the back of the truck, strange phenomena were going on inside my brain. I finally found out who I was, but I couldn't tell Julie that I knew my name. The connection wasn't yet being made between my mouth and brain. I didn't panic, but tried calmly to analyze what I was feeling.

Chapter 9

An Attempt at Recovery

alfway to Gillette we met the ambulance, and I was loaded into the back along with Bill, Julie and Bud. No one said anything. At the hospital, Bud and I were briefly evaluated and sent for tests and X-rays.

After what seemed hours, the emergency room physician said to me, "Due to the severe nature of your head injury, you should be taken to a more comprehensive medical facility."

I knew I was in no position to object. I was taken by Medivac helicopter to Natrona County Hospital in Casper, Wyoming. I was upset because I could not enjoy the helicopter ride. My focus was completely disarranged.

Waiting to greet me in the hospital emergency room was a neurosurgeon who soon determined that I should spend several days in the hospital.

The hospital stay was a continuation of the nightmare — four days of misery. I was drugged but still in terrible pain. Any little noise was very irritating, and I had no appetite. My entire body ached with any move I made. I wanted to sleep, but the crash tormented me. If I had died after losing consciousness, I wouldn't have known it. Death would have been peaceful. To make matters worse, I was there without the support of relatives and friends, and I couldn't see well because my glasses had been destroyed during the numerous impacts with the instrument panel. After what seemed like weeks, though only days, I was allowed to go home.

Bud and Anne flew down in a C-182 to pick me up — but not before the FAA had a chance to question me about the accident. The FAA was unpretentious to work with; they understood that I was not myself and was still in a vast amount of pain. The ride home was turbulent. Anne was dodging a tornado reported to be in the area, and Bud was in no condition to assist. I sat despondent in the back seat, wondering if I could fly again — or if I wanted to.

When we landed in Billings, I went inside Lynch, the local FBO, and noticed the employees there staring at me. After getting home and looking in the mirror I understood why. My face was swollen and moon-like. I had two black eyes, miscellaneous cuts and scratches, and under the bandages surrounding my forehead was the quarter-size wound where the flesh was completely gone.

"Oh, my God," I said to Anne, "there's no skin there, just mush. Will it ever be the same again?"

Anne, a registered nurse before she started her aviation career, assured me it would heal but was reluctant to predict what it might look like in the future.

The future — it scared me to think about it. Would my face look the same? How was I going to pay the hospital and doctor, over and above what medical insurance covered? Could I fly again? What about my career in food service management?

For days I stayed confined to my dinky attic apartment. I did not feel like driving, and I wasn't sure I could. Finally

I decided the best thing I could do was return to work, even though I felt bad. I had pushed myself in the past and it worked, I could do it again.

After several weeks of recovery time, I returned to work, and the problems began. I could not remember the location of items in the kitchen, I was tired and couldn't think. I had trouble making it through an eight-hour day. Irritable and bitchy, I made life miserable for my co-workers, my assistant manager and my friend, Julie.

My supervisor Roger noticed a big change in my attitude, capabilities and patience. I continued to force myself to go to work, pushing through day after day because I feared for my job and career. I told myself I must swiftly overcome the effects of this head injury and get on with my life. Meanwhile, I consulted a local neurosurgeon who prescribed drug therapy. With the addition of drugs, it became even more difficult for me to maintain a normal life.

Shortly after the crash, I was visited by an insurance adjuster at work. He assured me that the aviation insurance company would take care of any costs associated with my hospital stay and the follow-up doctor visits. After some time passed, however, Natrona County Hospital, where I was hospitalized in Casper, threatened to sue me for non-payment.

Mike Majerus, an attorney I consulted following the warning, was patient, sensitive and compassionate — well above the call of duty. Mike, a handsome, intelligent man, felt he could help me seek payment from the aviation insurance company. After leaving his office, I felt relieved. At least the nagging bills were no longer on my mind. Instead of my life getting better, though, it slowly started to unravel.

One Saturday morning, while helping restock the walk-in freezer at work, a three-gallon tub of ice cream fell off the top shelf and landed on my head directly where I'd been hurt in the airplane crash. The injury sent me to the hospital emergency room, then back to my neurosurgeon. He placed me at once on disability/non-working status and increased drug therapy.

I was home, then, for what I thought would be a few weeks, which later turned into a few months, and eventually a whole year. During that time, I stayed in close contact with Mike Majerus and also consulted various doctors, a psychologist, physical therapists and others in an effort to hasten my recovery time. Nothing seemed to be working rapidly enough. I felt dull, foggy and stupid. I was having a lot of trouble adjusting to the changes which had occurred as a result of the airplane accident. I'd started having trouble reading; the words separated from each other, and I could not think as fast as before. Concentrating for any period of time was out of the question.

The aviation insurance company had not kept its promise to pay medical bills and continued to violate several Montana statutes relating to my case. I had no choice but to sue the insurance company. This went against all my principles. If only they'd done what they said, I would not have pursued them. The legal proceedings became complicated; there was a discovery phase, followed by depositions, then hearings in front of a magistrate in an effort to settle the case out of court. Finally, that day in front of the magistrate, a settlement was agreed upon by both parties.

Nearly two years had passed before the legal issues were resolved, and I was still dealing with physical, emotional and mental scars resulting from the crash.

Chapter 10
ElectricBride

I never thought a head injury would completely change my life, but it did. Even today I am still affected; my temper is shorter than before, and I sometimes find it hard to concentrate or to assimilate new information as rapidly as before the accident. I have since found out this is a common problem with many people who have had severe head injuries of this nature.

As much as I hated to admit it, I had another impairment. It took me years to deal with my new set of limitations and accept them. The injury also left me with a permanent scar on my forehead. During the two-year legal battle, I decided that for my mental and emotional health I needed some diversion, possibly a creative outlet for my stress-related tension.

While living in Spokane I'd had an idea about developing a lighted bridal veil as a non-traditional alternative to the otherwise boring wedding ceremony. Now, because I wasn't working, I had the time to research and develop this new idea. My doctors agreed that it would be good therapy and might speed my recovery.

Being a fairly good seamstress, but having no knowledge

about the making of bridal veils or how to work with electronic components, I started out at the fabric store in downtown Billings. I purchased a bridal head frame and enough bridal illusion for the veil. Next, I went to Radio Shack and asked about lights, wire, a soldering iron, solder, battery packs and slide switches. They sold me these along with a basic electronics manual.

After reading about electricity/electronics, I decided to start the project trying to wire the lights first, then incorporate them into the veil design. I first tried wiring the lights in series and suddenly realized soldering the lights to the wire and to each other was a two-handed task. The pen-sized soldering iron needed to heat the two wires, then the solder with flux included needed to be applied to the hot wires to join all pieces. Finally I found a way. I aligned the wires, held the soldering iron in my mouth, heated the wires and used my hand to apply the solder.

It was painstaking work at first, and I had to make adjustments. I soon found that, if I wrapped the wires around small nails attached to a thin board, their ends would stay in place and make working with them easier. Next, I added a scrap piece of fabric to the insulated plug wire extending from the top of the soldering iron and to the hard plastic frame of the iron itself, and I taped it into place, so I could hold it between my teeth. This was more comfortable and safer than before, since the plug wire wouldn't wear and shock my mouth.

The six-volt mini-lights I used for the veil needed some preparation, too. I had to take off their colored, plastic coating with polish remover, which was hard to do because they were so tiny. I began to realize that if the veils sold in numbers, I would eventually need production help.

After experimenting with the electronic components, I found I had to wire the lights parallel rather than in series. After wiring them, I took one of the wires from the string and soldered it to one of two battery packs. The other wire went to a petite slide switch so the lights could be turned off and on. I completed the circuit by attaching a wire from one battery pack to the other; then I placed the batteries in the holders, pushed the slide switch to the "on" position and — like magic — the lights glowed.

At that point I incorporated the lights into the traditional tiara-style wedding frame and then attached the veil to the frame. The end result was a crude but adequate sample, good enough to start getting some objective opinions on the idea. One of the first to see my invention was Anne. She thought it was a outstanding idea and that it would sell.

I showed it to my mother, the next time I visited Southern California, and she said to me, "Wow! I think you really have something here!"

My dad, however, thought it was silly and told me it had already been done.

Disregarding his cynicism, I returned to Montana with a new and exciting goal to pursue. It seemed just the project I needed to get my mind off my health and on to something positive.

My next step was to see what local bridal shops in and around Billings thought about the new bridal veil concept. I had a number of responses. Sometimes doors slammed in my face and other times I heard, "That's interesting and different."

My last stop was at Meri's Bridal Chalet in downtown

Billings, where I showed the veil to Meri Ferguson, the owner. She looked at it and said, enthusiastically, "That's the best thing I have seen in twenty-five years in the business. Make me one to sell!"

My persistence had finally paid off. I was excited! She helped me refine the veil design that she thought would sell.

Before long, my first marketable veil sold, and Meri requested more veils and additional designs. I went to work matching the veil designs to the dresses she had in stock, so she could sell package bridal deals. After a few months of successful sales for us both, Meri, always full of good ideas and optimism, suggested I get a patent.

After some research, I found a patent attorney, Art Urban, who had an exceptional statewide reputation and was located in Red Lodge, Montana, about 60 miles southwest of Billings, near the Beartooth Mountain range.

One of the first things he asked me was, "Are you selling your product?" He emphasized the importance of testing the marketplace before any patent proceedings were initiated and agreed to meet with me at my home to discuss it further. After I showed him the veil he agreed to start patent procedures.

In the meantime, he instructed me to research my project and see if it could be improved upon. I continued to make the veils for Meri, but I experimented with various battery packs, lights, light-emitting diodes, switches and wires. Work often became frustratingly slow as a result of my head injury. In the process, though, I refined my original electronic design, which seemed to work better than all the other options.

Meri and I continued to work closely together and

The ElectricBride veil.

developed a special, lasting friendship. She taught me nearly
everything about the bridal business, showed me how to
improve upon my sewing skills and explained secrets of

selling bridal apparel to all age groups. With everything else in my life being negative, I felt this was the only bright spot.

Meri also wrote one of her suppliers on the East Coast about the lighted veil, which I had named, "ElectricBride." Dick Dietrick, owner of Washington Millinery Supply in Derwood, Maryland, requested pictures of my veil designs. Several months passed after I obliged his request. One day, however, Meri called and asked me to hurry over to her shop. Dick Dietrick was there and wanted to meet the inventor of the lighted veil!

When I told him that I wanted to market the veils nationwide but did not want to produce them on a large scale, he felt we might be able to work out a deal where his company would manufacture and market my veils, and I would receive a percentage of the sale proceeds. He was not sure, though, if the electronic portion of my veil design could be produced inexpensively enough to make it cost competitive. He invited me to visit him in Derwood to work with his designers, factory personnel and marketing representatives, and to see if we could make the veils cost effective. What a lucky break!

Chapter 11
Beyond Billings

Time seemed to pass quickly between Dick's visit and the day I left for Maryland. When I arrived at Dulles International Airport, Dick and his wife Josie were there to meet me. It seemed a long drive before we reached their home, a stately English Tudor house bordering a golf course and country club, where I was their guest for a five-day stay.

Josie and Dick were gracious hosts and welcomed me into their home and place of business like I was family. The next day, the three of us were up early and on our way to Washington Millinery Supply.

The business was located in a semi-new industrial building in Gaithersburg, and I was fascinated by its layout. The building was divided into several sections – an office complex, an order department with computers at each station, and a workroom where the veils were manufactured. Then there were aisles and aisles of inventory, a dye room, the designer desk and a retail showroom.

I was allowed total freedom to see how each area operated. Seeing what supplies I had to work with stimulated my creative side. The sizable millinery inventory dazzled me, much the same way I was mesmerized with fancy sequined fabrics and crystal beads as a child in my grandmother's sewing workroom.

My first order of business was to work with the veil designer to see if we could incorporate the lights into the veil and at the same time keep it cost effective. I wanted to have three designs – a traditional tiara style, a wreath and a hat. We started with the wreath, and I showed one of the seamstress supervisors how to attach the lights, how to solder and use the other electronic components.

After a few samples were made, we determined that the addition of the lights added a half hour of labor to each design. By altering the materials somewhat, that is, using less expensive flowers, we were able to make the lighted veils as competitive as non-lighted types. Dick suggested a marketing technique he used often which was to make a low-cost, a medium-cost and a high-cost design.

I enjoyed the flexibility he allowed me in the design, manufacturing and marketing areas. I would determine the percentage of profit I would receive from each veil sold, and Dick would take the veils to leading markets. This arrangement would allow me to continue making veils for Meri but let Dick take care of the remainder of the country.

Dick took the veils to Atlanta, Dallas, Chicago, New York and Los Angeles – all the major bridal markets. In some of his showrooms, the veils were lighted and displayed in the window 24 hours per day. I was flattered that he was willing to give the veils top exposure. He said later that he was amused by selling the veils to buyers who liked the idea of something fresh and innovative, a surprise, as well, to their unsuspecting customers.

The best thing about the lights is that they are incorporated in the veil design and can't be seen until the user decides to turn them on. And since we'd worked to keep the cost down, lights came at no additional cost. The best of both worlds. The lights lasted about one hour on four batteries, so the bride had the option of turning them on at the beginning of the ceremony, after she was kissed by the groom, or for the first dance at the reception. I heard of some brides who had the song, *You Light Up My Life*, played as they walked down the isle with their heads aglow.

It was a month or so before the checks for my percentage of sales started to appear in the mailbox. I took that money to help pay for more bridal supplies, travel and patent expenses.

My patent was now at the pending stage, and Art Urban felt certain full patent would be granted soon. But for now, the time was right for me to promote the veils as much as I could and add any last minute changes to the patent application.

Anne and I flew, as I felt well enough, to various locations in Montana and Colorado, publicizing the veils. That served two purposes. One was to sell veils; the other was to get me back in an airplane again.

In August 1986, after nearly two years of dedication and hard work, I was awarded a patent for a lighted bridal headdress from the United States Patent and Trademark Office. I had set another goal and achieved it through tremendous persistence and with the help of a fine patent attorney.

For the next year and a half I continued with the veils, bought a horse, took racquetball lessons to further improve my game and continued to see doctors for the headaches I still suffered as a result of the airplane accident.

I thought that having a horse again might take my mind off my headaches and improve my physical stamina. The horse I bought was a four-year-old, registered paint mare named Classy Doc that had not "colored." Though somewhat new to the horse business and inexperienced with its terminology, I soon learned that the mare was half paint and half quarter horse. When a paint is bred with a horse that is not paint, there is a fifty-fifty chance the horse will be a solid color rather than having the characteristic large areas of white patches.

Classy was a medium-sized, well-mannered horse, nicely proportioned, with a pretty head and a white blaze on her face. She'd had a year of cutting-horse training in Bozeman, Montana, so she was exceedingly responsive to any cue the rider gave her. Though she was probably more horse than I was capable of handling, I wanted her anyway and felt I could learn with her as time went on.

Initially, I kept her at the stable where I purchased her and thought it was odd that Add, the owner, didn't have more horses boarded there. It was a shabby but easily accessible facility which included a large outdoor riding area, several rows of covered stables, an indoor boarding area — where Add kept his own horses — and an indoor arena. I boarded Classy there for about two months before moving her elsewhere.

Classy's care and grooming did not present too much trouble, although I did have to re-think a one-handed method of cleaning her hooves before each riding session. Her two back legs presented the biggest problem because she had a bad habit of leaning on the leg being held; this put

Classy Doc and Sheri in Billings, Montana, 1985.

additional weight on me as I held that leg. I knew this couldn't work well for either of us, so I gradually trained her to pivot her foot back and rest the edge of her hoof on the ground. Then I could use the hoof pick to clean and inspect the frog and surrounding area without having to hold her weight. The two front legs did not present a problem, so I held each leg in turn securely between my knees while I cleaned the frog.

The next hurdle was getting her saddled and ready to ride. I used a halter with a side snap so that most of the halter slipped on her head and was easily secured with the snap. I did not use a bit because she seemed responsive with a hackamore, which I placed over the halter. This arrangement wasn't pretty, but it was functional because she was secured by a lead rope until I was ready to ride.

Next came the blanket and saddle. The saddle, a western roping type, was a problem for me to lift up and place correctly on her back. I just did not have the strength to lift more than 40 pounds over my head. I remembered from having a horse before that the next best thing to do was to stand on a bale of hay, a box or tack trunk next to the horse, lift the saddle to about my waist, then onto her back. Classy's willingness to cooperate was also helpful.

Cinching the saddle in the correct place was not troublesome, and we were soon ready to ride. I often stood on the same hay bale to mount Classy as I did to saddle her.

Riding was play for me and good exercise for Classy. We rode in all types of weather from hot summer sun to belly-deep snow. She was a sport about almost everything except water.

Add changed his stable rules daily to suit his needs, and soon I'd had enough of him. I knew of another stable about seven miles west of Billings where I could board Classy at a moment's notice, so on a clear, cool day in April, Classy and I decided to "ride into the sunset" toward her new home.

We trotted down a busy street, made it past a stop sign and signal light, a gravel plant, down the road about a mile and a half before having to cross a large canal full of murky, rushing water. There she stopped short.

Every attempt I made to get her to cross the bridge above the canal didn't work. I was holding the reins when she suddenly backed up, yanking me forward to the ground. I rolled under the guard rail on the bridge and into the canal. Hitting the turbid, icy water was such an enormous shock that, upon surfacing, I couldn't catch my breath.

By then, motorists had stopped to offer assistance; one man offered me his hand to help me up the steep embankment. Classy, frightened by the chain of events, was nowhere to be found. I had gruesome thoughts that perhaps she had been hit by a car or a gravel truck.

The man who helped me out of the water had seen her running, full speed, toward the intersection we had just crossed and offered to take me to find her. On the corner of the intersection stood another man with Classy's reins in hand. I was relieved to see she was not harmed, but since I was slightly hypothermic and emotionally rattled, I knew we both wouldn't be able to continue to our destination. I called a friend who brought her horse trailer, loaded us both and went on to Classy's new home. It was much better for both Classy and me to be at the new stable; it was out in the country with much more open riding area.

As I became slightly healthier, I started working with Anne on three new pilot ratings – instrument, commercial and certified flight instructor ratings – all of which moved me closer to professional pilot status. Progress was slow because I was still having trouble studying and assimilating new material.

I pushed myself, once again, to review the written test material over and over. To obtain any new rating it is necessary to pass oral, written and practical tests. The latter is performed with either a designated examiner or an FAA inspector, depending on the rating sought. By February of 1987, I had four additional ratings – an instrument, commercial, certified flight instructor and instrument instructor – and was ready to pursue a career in aviation. Even though I was plagued by headaches, which I was told might be lifelong, I was healthy enough to pass a second-class medical exam.

During my checkrides for the additional ratings, I asked the designated examiner, Gary Wolterman, an accomplished pilot himself, if he thought a multi-engine rating might be an option for me. He thought about it a minute and said in a promising tone, "I think having two legs is more important than two arms." He went on to explain that throughout multi-engine training the student, usually flying a simple, underpowered, multi-engine airplane, learns to fly it on one engine. During critical phases of flight, including the takeoff roll, rotation, climb and landing procedures, a pilot learns to handle adverse yaw caused by differential thrust. Meaning, one engine running, the other not.

I set out to locate a school that would teach me how to fly a multi-engine airplane, hoping to add that credit to my certificate. It didn't take long to find what I wanted, and in less than 10 hours, I had a multi-engine rating. It was effortless to obtain, and my lack of an arm never was a restriction to the process.

I began to send my "low-time" résumé around the country, looking for a position as a commercial pilot/flight instructor. I had several enticing offers, including one for flying in Alaska to spot herring. It was my understanding that one day a year, near Bristol Bay, the fishermen were allowed to catch herring. Aircraft were used to spot the schools of fish from the air, then direct the fishermen on the bay to that site. The second job offer was flying tours up and down the coast in North Carolina, near Kitty Hawk. The third job was giving flight instruction in Lexington, Kentucky. I finally chose the job in Lexington. After all, the flight school was operated by a woman, I wanted to experience the culture of the southeast, and Lexington was horse country.

Chapter 12
Teasing Fate

I decided it would be best to visit Aero-Tech, the only
flight school on Bluegrass Field in Lexington – possibly
my next employer – and see if I liked the surrounding
area. It was about the second week in February, 1987, when
I arrived in Lexington. I got along well with Arlynn, the
owner/operator, and there was a variety of aircraft on hand
for both teaching and flying.

After two separate checkrides over two days, to show her
I was capable of flying both right and left seat with one arm,
Arlynn was satisfied, and I was hired as a flight instructor
on the spot. She assigned me several students and had me
flying Valentine's Day champagne flights.

These champagne flights carried one couple, who were
given the back seat of a C-172, a bottle of champagne, and
a half hour of flight time with me as their pilot. I would take
off with the couple, and their chilled bottle, and slowly fly
over the city of Lexington at night.

While I was still in town, working and waiting to return
to Billings to gather my personal belongings, I got my first
taste of southern hospitality. My first few nights in Lexington I spent in the home of Mr. and Mrs. Tom Collins, Jr.,

whose son, Tom III, was an attorney and a flight instructor at Aero-Tech. His parents were vacationing in Florida through the damp Kentucky winter, and I had the house completely to myself.

Immense, elegant, with typical southern architecture and complete with period antiques, the house sat on a horse farm located on the outskirts of the city. Tom stayed in a guest house at the edge of the property; he became my first friend and offered assistance and support with my new job.

After a week's stay in Lexington, I returned to Billings and hurriedly made arrangements to pack and drive to my new home. I decided that, as long as I was single, I could keep my mobile home in Billings as a "base camp" and travel at will. My mother wanted to come with me to help with the three-day drive and see more of America. We shared the driving, stopped as we wished and arrived in Lexington on schedule so I could start my new job.

Once I had started my job, my next priority was to find a place to live. At first I stayed at a lovely bed and breakfast in Versailles, six miles west of Lexington. But I found a furnished basement apartment in Lexington, not far from the airport, that had all the comforts of home and was in a safe neighborhood beneath a family of four. My hours at the airport were so long that I was only home to sleep, so it worked out fine. I had finally achieved another of my goals — to work in aviation and get paid for flying. It was a stimulating time in my life; I worked diligently with my students and had a better-than-90-percent pass rate with private and instrument candidates. It was not uncommon for me to fly 100 hours a month or more and have over 25 students at one time.

Before long, I was flying and teaching in every type of aircraft on the flight line. When I was not flying due to poor weather, I spent my time getting to know the other pilots who worked at the flight school. They were a fun-loving group who were willing to share various hangar stories and flight instructor techniques.

I felt I had a unique method of teaching that actually helped students learn to plan and "stay ahead" of the aircraft. I often laughed with students at myself, explaining that they were learning the one-handed way of flying.

Though difficult for me to actually show, I insisted that students put one hand on the yoke, the other on the throttle during critical phases of flight, takeoffs and landings, or during the practice of maneuvers. I insisted on talking on the ground, which included a thorough pre-flight briefing of maneuvers so there would be less talking over the engine at altitude. I showed students what happened to pitch after engine power was applied and reduced and the effect of flaps, gear and other control surfaces. I emphasized that, by knowing these flight characteristics, each student had no excuse for allowing a massive pitch down after power is significantly reduced.

By planning ahead, concentrating and knowing the particular training aircraft, a student should be basically "hands free." Though I've proved flying is not necessarily two-handed, working smarter — mentally — is a significant advantage to any pilot.

I was amazed that I never had one student question my ability to fly with one arm. Initially I thought this might be an issue and tried to prepare myself for questions of this nature with every new student.

After a year of flight instruction I had one student mention her particular thoughts on my role as the instructor. She said to me, "Sheri, do you realize I am putting my life in your hand? Here we are, virtual strangers and I am going up with you in a small aircraft."

I realized at that moment this idea was of equal importance to me. It was possible to have an occasional student show evidence of near panic. As a flight instructor, I watched each student carefully for signs of acute nervousness to avoid any potential panic situations. For them, as it was for me at one point in my training, an adverse experience could lead to the loss of a student.

Unfortunately, there were anxious moments for me as an instructor. On one instructional flight, I was teaching the practice of power-off stalls to a low time student pilot. This is a maneuver where you purposely stall the aircraft, then recover from the resultant loss of lift. During the practice of these stalls, my jittery student panicked, held the airplane in a stall, yoke fully extended in his lap, and simultaneously applied full left rudder deflection. This provoked an involuntary spin entry. In an instant, the world was spinning rapidly, and the ground loomed larger.

"Let go of the yoke!" I requested firmly.

There was no response from the student, only a continued, frozen stance with a wide-eyed stare out the windscreen.

I reached up and abruptly smacked the top side of my yoke in a downward motion. At the same time I repeated my request — in a *shrill* tone of voice.

Running out of altitude quickly, my next move was to physically whack the sizeable male student; but, he let go.

Instantaneously, I recovered from the spin, using a forward motion on the yoke and opposite rudder deflection, then pulled out of the ensuing dive.

Slightly shaken, I got my bearings and proceeded from the practice area back to Lexington. It wasn't long thereafter that the student terminated flight training. Knowing his prior history of excitability, I didn't discourage him.

One of the pilots who always seemed to be in the lobby at Aero-Tech, waiting for a job call, was Joe Marshall. Joe, originally from Louisville, Kentucky, was a commercial pilot, working on his flight instructor rating, and he had built many of his hours flying ferry trips.

Arlynn sent her airplanes to separate locations for maintenance after hours, and Joe and I would ferry these aircraft on a regular basis. One of us would fly the aircraft needing maintenance, the other in a chase plane. After dropping the aircraft off, we came back to Lexington together in the chase plane. The flying done for the day, we often had a late dinner together.

Joe was young, handsome, sociable and exciting to be with. His aviation goal was to become an airline pilot. We became good friends and started to date more seriously. Our love of flying was a very strong bond. I was growing more attached to Joe, more so than I knew at the time. One night, on a ferry flight, Joe began having trouble with his aircraft. There were three pilots flying that night: Joe, myself and Bobby Allen. We were ferrying airplanes south of Lexington to Madison airport for maintenance. I was in a Cessna 172, Bobby in a Piper Arrow and Joe in a Cessna 152.

Joe had recently been enthralled with how well the little trainers rolled, and, when the occasion presented itself, he tried his skills at aerobatics. This night, though, as Joe rolled the airplane, there was just not enough momentum to get the craft over the top of the turn. As he rolled out of the maneuver, he managed to get slightly negative, and after resuming a level flight attitude, he realized that his ailerons (control surfaces controlling the roll rate of the aircraft) were stuck in a right-turn position.

The three of us monitored the same radio frequency, and Bobby and I heard Joe say, "Bobby, my ailerons are stuck!"

We acknowledged his transmission but felt helpless.

Joe took the yoke with both hands and turned it hard to the left in an attempt to straighten the turning aircraft. This worked to straighten his flight path, but the ailerons were still immobile. His only choice was to rely on his rudder to yaw the airplane the direction in which he wanted to turn. Madison airport seemed to frequently have a direct crosswind, so Joe decided to divert to Aero-Tech's other maintenance facility in Danville, Kentucky. He knew that, without the complete use of all his control surfaces, dealing with a crosswind might cause him to lose directional control and veer off the runway.

Bobby and I continued on to Madison, dropped off the other Cessna and went in the Piper Arrow to Danville after Joe. Meanwhile, Joe made a precarious landing at Danville without any further complications.

After Bobby and I landed at Danville a short time later, we discovered that Joe and a mechanic had located the problem. After removing an inspection plate under the wing, they found a riveting tool lodged between the bell crank and the push rod assembly of the aileron. It had accidently been left in the wing by a mechanic after some airframe/rivet work had been completed some seven years earlier. When Joe experienced negative G forces during the aileron roll that evening, the tool had dislodged itself from where it had been left years ago. This incident was the turning point in our relationship.

From then on, we cherished our time together more. Joe and I both realized how vulnerable and fragile life was and how quickly events could change it. We also agreed that obeying FAA rules was one of the key issues to staying alive. The respect we had for aviation, aircraft and our pilot training was more ingrained by this chain of events.

Joe and I learned to scuba dive the summer of 1987. It was something we both wanted to do, and another one of those goals I had set for myself and wanted to complete.

Our diving instructor was Richard Huber, also a pilot, a commercial student of mine and a good friend. As we started into the diving program I did not think it was difficult. Richard had assured me he thought I could be a diver with one arm. I would still have to prove I could complete all the requirements to get certified. I didn't have much concern until I got to the "ditch and don" stage, when I nearly drowned myself.

During "ditch and don," I was instructed to attach my mask to my pre-checked scuba gear, then told to throw the gear into the deep end of the pool. After diving into the pool, I was to swim down to the gear, place the regulator in my mouth, put the mask on and clear it, then "don" the scuba gear and swim to the surface.

Richard had been conscientious about instructing, then letting us try various phases of any task so we were not unprepared. I proceeded with the ditch and don, swam down to my gear, put the regulator in my mouth, but I had trouble keeping my body from floating to the surface while I put on my mask. It was nearly impossible for me to breath only through the regulator in my mouth without water going up my nose.

I struggled to keep everything under control and couldn't. Water went up my nose, down my throat, and I panicked. I popped up to the surface, unable to talk and very upset, as I realized I had failed this first attempt at donning my equipment. Richard was patient and suggested I calm myself and try again; this time he would let me put on my mask first, and then go after the remainder of the gear.

Once again I swam down to the scuba gear, put the regulator in my mouth, then, as quickly as I could, I put the buoyancy compensator (BC) jacket and tank on my back and attached the plastic clips at the front. I had done it.

After finishing the pool portion of the instruction, it was time for open water dives, which we completed at Key West, Florida. Diving in salt water was much better than the fresh water pool and had many more intriguing distractions. As we dove in and around the jagged coral reefs, there seemed to be an endless variety of animals and plant life. The colors ranged from bright aqua, orange and purple to mysterious maroon. It was not unusual for silvery barracuda bearing fine, sharp teeth to follow us, all the time inspecting each move we made. We inadvertently scared lobster, minus claws, farther back in their crevices. We awed at the sight of miniature sharks and were painfully stung by fire coral, which was appropriately so named. After two exciting dives we were certified and ready to go with our dive buddy. Diving is a sport that should not be missed by anyone who appreciates swimming and enjoys the splendor, color and animals of the world beneath the sea.

Joe and I were best dive buddies; I could depend on him to stay close, making the dive a glorious experience for both of us. It was apparent that scuba diving was another interest we shared and a sport we both love

Chapter 13
Love at Last

Joe and I were spending a lot of time together, and it wasn't long before he asked me to move in with him so that we could be together day and night. I agreed, although I expressed some apprehension. What if it didn't work out? What if working and living together proved to be too much?

Relationships in the past had been somewhat checkered, and I never really knew if, in the back of the mind of any of my previous boyfriends, he really accepted me as I was, with my single arm. Though I didn't date or had never been invited to a prom in high school, I dismissed it as a lack of maturity on the part of the guys.

After high school and on through college, though, meeting men was still perplexing. I never was asked on a blind date, and sometimes I felt I was passed up for the girl with two arms but a whole lot fewer brains. After my breakup with Rick, I had attempted to meet suitable men in night-clubs and ran into shallow alcoholics who were interested in one-night stands. The emphasis seemed to be on physical looks.

As much as friends loved me and accepted me, they were

reluctant to introduce me to their single male friends. Part of their reluctance was my having one arm; the other was because they knew I was very particular about the men I dated. Although selective, I occasionally became involved in situations which caused me to wonder if I wanted to date at all.

During my early twenties I was involved with a support group whose members were amputees. The name of the group said it all — Amputees in Motion, AIM, for short. The group concentrated on keeping amputees involved in athletic pursuits, mainly skiing.

The premier ski event of the year was an amputee competition in Winter Park, Colorado. I was the only arm amputee in the group, the remainder being twelve to fifteen leg amps who referred to themselves casually as "gimps."

There was one member who was not an amputee but who lent his support to the group and their activities. After attending several meetings, this man asked me to his home for dinner, and I graciously accepted, even though I wasn't attracted to him physically in the least.

We talked about a variety of subjects, including future AIM events. However, as the evening progressed, he explained how and why he was involved with the group. I was unnerved when he said he was very attracted *to women who had lost limbs!* As my stomach was turning, he explained away his intrigue by saying it was like any other attribute a woman might possess — for example, blonde hair or green eyes. I never thought having one arm was anything BUT negative and found it repulsive that he liked me for that reason. I thought he was mentally sick — he even referred to himself as a "monopedimaniac," a term he'd picked up from reading the latest issue of *Hustler*. I couldn't wait to get away from him and left shortly thereafter. My interest in the group began to wane, and since I hadn't planned to compete in skiing, I quit.

For years I'd sought someone like Joe who had the qualities I was looking for — a sense of humor, a career goal, similar interests to mine, intellect and a zest for life. I'm glad I didn't settle for less, just to be able to say I was married, but waited until I was sure. This man loved me for what was inside, not how I looked on the outside. He was attracted to me because I was able to do more and was more motivated than those with two arms. He marveled at my flying ability, other talents, gregarious personality and energetic plans for the future.

It was a major gamble for me to live with Joe, but I decided to take a chance. It had been a while since I had a serious relationship, and even if it didn't last, perhaps I would be a better person after the experience. Our relationship continued to get stronger, however, and we started to make plans for a future together.

In October, after living together for over six months, we decided to announce our engagement. It was short, only two months — barely enough time to make arrangements for the wedding. We decided to marry the week before Christmas at Joe's father's home in Louisville. The ceremony would be brief, performed by a justice of the peace, with only the family invited, and the reception would be open to friends. While wedding plans were taking place, we also decided to buy a home in Lexington.

Although I had purchased several houses in the past, this was the first I'd acquired with another person. The house was in a proper section of town, near the University of Kentucky and close to shopping. Over forty years old, it was a brick Cape Cod with three bedrooms, bath and a half, full basement, garage and ample yard. There were uneven-width pine floors throughout, a large kitchen and a small breakfast nook which we felt added to the home's charm. As both our wedding and escrow closing dates approached, the stress began to take its toll on me, however, more than on easy-going Joe. I suffered from intense headaches and a bad case of nervousness. As it turned out, though, we were able to move into our home and get semi-settled a week before the wedding.

After days of preparation and months of planning, the wedding day finally arrived. Everything was in place, and I felt emotionally relieved to have the arrangements over with. At this point I was ready to have the wedding behind me, and for Joe and me to get on with our new life together. My family had arrived from California just the day before; Joe's dad let me decorate the house with pine ropes, wreaths, flowers and other Christmas decorations. The caterers, harpist and cake came, ready for the huge event.

As much as I wanted a grand bridal bouquet, I realized how awkward it would be to hold flowers and, at the same time, shake the hands of well wishers. The answer was a wristlet of white roses combined with seasonal greenery and a red bow. Meri sent me a beautiful white wedding dress — imported, with beads and pearls on it — and I made my own headpiece, a lighted wreath veil complete with beautiful iridescent and silk flowers and imported Austrian crystal beading.

As my father and I walked down the stairs toward the

Joe and Sheri on their wedding day, December 19, 1987.

spacious living room, I switched on the veil and could hear the oohs and aahs. In front of the lavishly decorated mantle, Joe and the justice of the peace waited for me. Joe was handsome in his tux with a red tie and cummerbund.

The ceremony was brief, and after pictures, hugs and

kisses, we celebrated through the evening. Joe suggested we spend our honeymoon night in our new home, so we drove to Lexington after the reception. The next day my family drove to Lexington to spend time with us before returning to California. We enjoyed Christmas together before flying ourselves to our official honeymoon at Longboat Key, Florida.

In Florida we spent a week in a condominium on the beach overlooking the Gulf of Mexico. We had thought we might go scuba diving but chose instead to do very little except enjoy each other's company.

Being newlyweds was great, but even though we'd lived together, there were adjustments to be made in our everyday life. Sharing a checkbook, the bathroom, household chores, grocery shopping and cooking required some compromises. Now I had to suit another person, as well as myself. The commitment of marriage was there to bind us, however, when either of us became upset enough to leave. We seemed to work out the problem and go on with our lives. I appreciated and loved Joe more and more as time went on. I found a genuine, honest man with whom I could share my life — something which often inspired me to count my blessings.

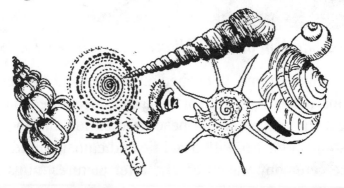

Flight Through Life

Obtain a good briefing
    before departure each day.
Preflight yourselves
    to make sure your mental and
    physical conditions are up to each
    day's journey.
Maintain communications
    with each other at all times.
Set your course and follow it;
    but remain flexible in order to be able
    to navigate around the storms of life.
Pay attention to the warnings
    of cumulus buildup so as not to
    become trapped in a large storm cell.
Avoid all icing conditions.
And lastly,
    may both of you have a safe and
    pleasant journey, take time to enjoy
    the sights along the way, and may the
    God of Life provide you with a
    constant tail wind.

This poem was written by Joe C. Marshall, Jr., M.D. and dedicated to Joe and me at our wedding ceremony.

Chapter 14

The Alaska Quest

As Joe and I continued with our aviation careers, we occasionally had to be apart, and we found that our love for each other was even more apparent during these times.

One summer, when we were both working for Aero-Tech, I chose to fly a group of students to Alaska for a two-week adventure. I had heard time and again from other pilots that it just couldn't be done in a single-engine airplane and in visual flight conditions.

It took Arlynn, the group leader, several months to complete all the detailed plans for this trip. She did the flight planning and weight and balance calculations for every leg (which included a change of seats for all but the senior pilots who stayed with their particular aircraft). She chose the airports of intended landing, made the hotel and rental car reservations, planned the side excursions, saw to it that the aircraft to be used on the trip had fresh 100-hour inspections, ordered instrument charts for each senior pilot and kept up the enthusiasm of the individuals with frequent meetings of those who were to go on the trip.

There were three aircraft — a Piper Twin Seneca, a Lance

and a Turbo Arrow. I flew the Lance most of the way. There were 12 people taking part in this adventure: the three senior pilots (myself, Arlynn and Charlie), seven other pilots who wanted to build cross-country time, and two non-pilots.

The departure day arrived, and we were given a big send-off by wellwishers. The first leg of the trip, which started late in the afternoon, was from Lexington to Des Moines, Iowa, where we would spend the night. We departed and were in either visual or radio contact with each other most of the time. Although flight conditions were poor — three miles in haze — we wanted to fly the entire trip VFR (visual flight rules), if at all possible.

The leg progressed normally until just east of Springfield, Illinois, where I flew directly into a thunderstorm. I did several tasks as promptly as possible: first, I had to fly the airplane and not allow the lightning to distract me; second, execute a change of course north, away from the storm, in an attempt to stay VFR, knowing a 180-degree course change was out of the question because Charlie was following behind me in the Seneca; third, obtain an IFR clearance (clearance to fly in instrument conditions) from the nearest FAA center agency with radar coverage of that area. If I asked for a clearance from the center agency, they would assist me in resuming an on-course heading westbound and, at the same time, use their radar coverage to help me pick my way around any additional thunderstorms.

I might add at this point that, from a pilot's perspective, thunderstorms, however intense, should be avoided. They often contain dangerous up and down drafts, blinding lightning, hail that can damage airframes by pitting leading edges of wings, or in the worst case, remove the paint down to the bare aluminum.

After dealing with these three tasks, I had a final one —
to offer assistance to one of the non-pilots, sitting in the front
seat next to me, who was throwing up. I was busy, to say the
least, staying safe, legal and nursing a sick passenger. After
another hour we landed, without any further episodes, in
Des Moines.

The next day we flew northwest, low over the Badlands
of South Dakota for a close look at the colorful formations
and landed at Rapid City, South Dakota. From there, we
visited Mt. Rushmore and ate lunch while looking up at the
overwhelming faces carved in the mountainside. That afternoon we departed Rapid City, flew west over several
mountain ranges and into Jackson, Wyoming, at dusk. We
stayed in the Jackson area for a few days, and while the
remainder of the group visited the Tetons and Yellowstone
National Parks, I took the Lance north to Billings, Montana,
to check on my mobile home's condition and to see friends.
After I returned to Jackson a day later, we all departed
northwest-bound again, with a lunch stop in Pendleton,
Oregon.

Vancouver, British Columbia, was our final destination
for that day, after a very scenic flight through the Columbia
Gorge and northward over the Seattle area. The next day we
departed north toward Port Hardy, B.C., enjoying clear
weather, which allowed us to see several large cruise ships
voyaging up the spectacular inside passage. After a fuel stop
in Port Hardy, we were back in the air again, flying above the
Queen Charlotte Islands and navigating mostly by pilotage,
that is, comparing the landscape below to a sectional chart
in hand. To our right appeared Prince Rupert and finally

Ketchikan, where we spent the night.

I enjoyed Ketchikan from an aviation point of view because the land airport parallels a canal where the sea-planes land and depart. This same canal separates the airport from the city of Ketchikan, which is perched on a narrow portion of land between the sea and mountains. The next day we were dealing with some of Alaska's infamous poor weather, a low ceiling and one- to two-mile forward visibility in fog and light rain. After talking to several local pilots about a suitable route of flight to follow in order to stay VFR, we departed for St. Petersburg and our next fuel stop.

After leaving St. Petersburg, flying no higher than 400 or 500 feet off the ocean surface, we noticed large chunks of aqua-blue ice floating on top of the saltwater to our right. As we got closer, we saw what seemed like a wall of craggy aqua ice – our first glacier sighting! We continued to thread our way at low altitude through islands toward Gustavus. The steep-sided land masses rose out of the water like inverted ice cream cones. The tops of these formations were obscured by fog.

I knew, if the weather continued to deteriorate, we could always turn back to St. Petersburg. The pilots on board with me were apprehensive about the weather. They knew as well as I did that filing an instrument flight plan was out of the question because the minimum *en route* altitudes for terrain clearance, as well as radar coverage from Center, were above the freezing level. I didn't want to take a chance of accumulating airframe ice. Fortunately for us, the weather started to break up slightly, allowing us to make a visual approach into Gustavus.

To get from the airport to the lodge required a lengthy bus ride on a gravel road, which was continuously lined with pine trees, dense ferns and bushes. We spent the night there and for the first time realized it did not get dark. Kaye, my roommate, was walking alone in the woods surrounding the lodge at midnight and found a huge mound of fresh bear excrement. She realized at that moment how vulnerable she was to the threat of wild animals and hastily retreated to the lodge.

We returned the next day to the airport and departed with good weather for a sensational view of Glacier Bay. It was a dramatic sight, flying up-close to glaciers, then viewing several whales in the crystal-clear, deep blue water while *en route* to Juneau. We found Juneau to be a busy beehive of aviation activity with land and sea planes constantly coming and going. That afternoon we boarded one of two sailboats and headed out on the bay to see wildlife and enjoy a fresh salmon bake.

Our next day's flight farther north required us to fly up a narrow canyon with an overcast ceiling, which obscured the mountaintops on either side. We entered an open area with glacial-fed Kluane Lake below, and beyond the lake we crossed swampy, tundra-like terrain before reaching Northway. Our original route of flight would have taken us over the ocean to Cordova and then Anchorage, but unsatisfactory weather, including icing conditions, precluded that flight plan.

After a fuel stop and weather briefing in Northway, we followed the Alaska Highway over Gulkana where I began to have electrical problems with the Lance. I suspected an alternator failure so, in order to reserve what battery might be left, I shut off everything in the cockpit that required electrical power. We continued on, still in VFR flight conditions, into Merrill Field at Anchorage. On board the Lance was a hand-held radio, which allowed me to contact the control tower at Merrill Field for a landing clearance. While we were in Anchorage for a few days, the certified mechanic at the fixed-based operator worked on the Lance's electrical problems.

Our precious few days to sightsee in Anchorage went by swiftly. We took a train to Denali National Park, and it was one of those rare days when we could see Mt. McKinley – no clouds to obscure the glorious view. After returning to Anchorage, we attended a dinner in our honor, hosted by the local chapter of the 99s, of which Arlynn, Kaye and I were members.

The next day it was time to depart again for Northway, on to Haines Junction, down the Alcan Highway and over to Whitehorse for lunch and a fuel stop. Once again I encountered electrical problems. The Lance was not yet repaired!

Just east of Teslin, Yukon Territory, we encountered an unexpected thunderstorm with instrument flight conditions, so we returned to Teslin and landed on the gravel strip to wait out the storm. After the storm had passed, we departed for Watson Lake, landed and spent the night. We stayed an extra day there because of the Lance's electrical problems. We knew we would need to leave Watson Lake on an instrument flight plan, due to instrument weather conditions, and would require electrical power for navigational equipment and radio communications.

After repairs were made, we departed Watson Lake on an ADF airway (automatic direction finder, a type of navigational equipment that uses low frequency or AM radio waves) outside of radar coverage *en route* to Dawson Creek. From Dawson Creek it was on to Calgary, where we spent our next night. From that point forward to Fargo, North Dakota, and then home to Lexington, it was uneventful.

We were glad to be home. I was glad to get out of the cockpit after over 60 hours of flight time. The two weeks we were gone seemed like two years, but we had accomplished much in a short time. We did what everyone thought was impossible — fly a single-engine plane that far and back again without any serious mishaps or delays. We also learned to deal with Canadian and U.S. customs, studied the proper use of survival equipment (although we didn't need to use it) in flight emergencies, and to professionally handle unforecast or deteriorating weather conditions. For me, and for those pilots to whom I gave dual instruction in the cockpit of the Lance, and for our non-pilot passengers, it was the experience of a lifetime.

Chapter 15
Glennis Arie

A fter returning from the Alaska trip, Joe and I decided we couldn't stand to be away from each other for that length of time again. I never thought of him or myself as the clingy type, but the time and distance we'd been apart had an impact on us. We continued on with our aviation careers. Joe went to work as an on-demand charter pilot at Haps Aerial Enterprises, Clark County Airport in Sellersburg, Indiana, across the river from Louisville, almost a two-hour drive from Lexington.

Though this job was inconvenient and didn't pay enough, we both understood it would put him closer to an airline job. In order to make ends meet, I went back to work full-time as a food service manager. As I continued to flight instruct part-time, I was also hired as co-director of food service at Eastern State Hospital, a state-managed hospital for the mentally retarded and mentally ill. It had an ancient but spacious kitchen facility that fed more than 350 patients at one time.

I was responsible for supervising three dining halls, though all the food was prepared in the main kitchen and transferred to the satellite kitchens. The patients who were on their best behavior were allowed to walk down to the cafeteria and eat; the others were confined to the ward. I had a staff of approximately 35, mostly black, and all seemed to accept and like me as their supervisor.

It was the first time I had worked with a kitchen crew that was nearly all black. I was afraid there would be problems dealing with them because I was white, physically impaired and their new manager. The crew had been there much longer than I and knew the routine; I didn't.

As with any new food service management position in the past, I started out asking questions, asking for assistance and being non-aggressive. I quickly realized that by asking for their help and communicating the required events for the day and week, we were able to produce timely results that were appreciated by both staff and patients. I became very attached to the kitchen staff, which made leaving the hospital, several months later, emotionally trying.

Since I had never been around mental patients before, the precautions we had to take seemed strange to me, though I realized they were important. Hot beverages or foods were never served *very* hot because, often, the medication the patients took had numbing effects. Apparently the patients couldn't judge temperature well and could easily burn themselves. Plastic silverware was sent to the wards to protect patients from injuring themselves and others. One dining hall, which served mostly mentally retarded patients, was kept locked as were a majority of the wards. On one floor there was a double-locked facility, meaning it was necessary to pass through two doors, which housed the violent or unpredictable mentally ill. I never went there unescorted. Patients were never allowed in the main kitchen — for safety reasons. If one or two accidentally made an appearance, Miss Lucy, the senior supervisor, would run them off. The kitchen knives were always hidden after the work day was over.

Each quarter, my co-director, Thelma, and I would visit the wards and take a patient-food survey. One patient very seriously told us, "The food ,overall, is good, but I can do without the baby snakes." I could not keep from laughing. We both assumed he was referring to spaghetti. Another patient asked me where my right arm was, and I explained I lost it as a child. He said, "Well, get another one." I asked him, "How do I do that?" He said, with a crazed look, "Ask the doctor!"

Nearly a year had passed since Joe started commuting to Sellersburg, and we decided it would be best to relocate to Louisville. I had also been hired full-time with an engineering firm that conducted aerial surveys out of Clark County Airport, where Joe was based. We rented our house in Lexington and bought another in Louisville, near Cherokee Park, a historic area. The house was a two-story, 76-year-old frame house with three bedrooms, attic and full basement.

At this same time it became evident that I was pregnant with our first child. For years I had mixed feelings about having a child. I had been around the children of friends and relatives and thought it wasn't for me. I wasn't too worried about the physical obstacles, but dealing with a child, emotionally, was another matter. Did I want the hassles, the joy, the responsibility? As I entered my early thirties, something inside me changed regarding child bearing. I could no longer live with indecision. Now that I had a secure marriage and Joe desired children, we were both elated that I was pregnant. We looked forward to our life as a family.

Three months pregnant and flying a Piper Twin Comanche doing aerial surveys.

For the first few months following our move to Louisville, I worked as a pilot/photographer for the engineering firm flying aerial surveys. I learned from my co-captain, Jim, about the survey business and took pride in being able to take acceptable black and white or color negatives with the nine-inch-square RC-8 camera. This large camera was mounted in the rear of the Twin Comanche cabin, which had a camera hole cut in its belly. Flying the Twin Comanche to and from jobs all over Kentucky was like flying a sports car.

After I flew to the job site, I would climb in the back and ready the camera to take pictures. Jim flew the airplane, following flight lines which were drawn on a map as a guide for the area to be photographed. This was often burdensome over sparsely populated or geographically nondescript areas, and I began to notice that, for Jim, flying the airplane seemed secondary to flying the flight lines. I began to get distressed about many of Jim's procedures while accompanying him in the aircraft.

After nearly four months of flying with him, my concern for our safety, my unborn child's safety and the company's liability, prompted me to write my supervisor a three-page letter complete with dates, times and the operating practices Jim followed, which – in my opinion – seemed improper. These included entering restricted airspace without proper clearance, a disregard for Federal Aviation Regulations, dangerous aircraft operating procedures and showing up for work smelling of alcohol. As much as I enjoyed the job, I resigned within six months.

Though I continued to work part-time as a flight instructor, my mind was on the baby growing inside me. My maternal instinct was strong, and I spent several months getting the nursery ready for our new arrival. I was more than half way through my pregnancy when I decided to wallpaper the nursery. I chose a pattern with tiny bears flying small red airplanes. *How perfect!* I thought. Until moving to Kentucky, I had never heard the expression, "Busier than a one-armed paper hanger." There really *is* some truth to it.

As a child I sat quietly while watching my mother wallpaper, so I called her first for advice. First I applied wallpaper preparation, a type of sealer, usually rolled or brushed on the wall to help the paper adhere. Next, I used a chalk line as a guide, so the wallpaper would hang straight. Since I am left-handed, I started from right to left, lining up the edge of the wallpaper to the chalk line. I made sure the paper was rolled up with the glue to the outside, and thoroughly soaked with water so the glue had a chance to activate before it was applied to the wall. Then, I started at the top of the chalk line, smoothing out part of the paper with a wet sponge. This part of the paper stayed in place while I aligned the bottom edge with the bottom of the chalk line. When the edge was straight I smoothed out the remaining paper with a sponge. After I was satisfied with the results, I used a sharp razor cutter to trim the top and bottom of the paper. Photos and text illustrating "one-armed paper hanging" are included in Part II of this book.

I've learned about several items that make the job easier, a sharp cutter blade, a steady ladder, measuring tape, a plastic tray to soak the wallpaper in and a paper that incorporates an overall, short, repeat pattern. After several days the nursery was complete, and I was thrilled with the results. Everyone saw my workmanship and wondered how I could paper so well with one arm. My answer was, as always, patience and persistence.

A few short months later, September 30, 1989, Glennis Arie Marshall, eight pounds, eight ounces, was born. My mother flew in from California to help me, and I'd done all I could to prepare for Glennis' homecoming.

After Glennis came home from the hospital with me, I began to have my doubts about how I was going to care for a child by using only one arm. I had made sure every baby product and piece of equipment I had purchased or was given was an item I could operate with one hand. The crib could be managed one-handed, with quiet side rails; the high chair was a swing-away tray type; and the car seat had a one-hand-operation-type buckle. I used cloth diapers at first, thinking I was helping the environment, and the plastic pants had Velcro™ closures. I later switched to disposable diapers due to Glennis' persistent diaper rash and found the tapes securing the diapers were equally easy to manage one-handed. Baby clothes were the type with zippers or snap fasteners and no small buttons, which would have been more time consuming.

A new baby must be picked up a certain way — with two hands. The baby's head is supported with the one hand, the other goes under the back and the bottom. Being careful not to allow the baby's head to bend backward is a primary concern when handling a child under three months of age. What worked out best for me was to grasp Glennis by the right side of her rib cage, and, as I picked her up, to roll her into my forearm, then over onto her stomach. It wasn't long before she had the hang of this maneuver and would assist me by starting to roll in that direction. I chose to breast feed at first and would lay her head and upper body on a pillow supported by a chair arm or additional pillows and place her close to my breast.

Dressing Glennis the first year was not an obstacle; she was agreeable to holding still and was patient with me. During "diaper changing time," she understood that it was not the time to roll over; in addition, I gave her something to play with while I changed her.

As I noticed she was getting more independent, I encouraged her to try dressing herself. As she started to see more of what I did in a day's time, she wanted to help. Getting her to the stage where we could finally communicate with each other was a huge milestone. She understood what I said far earlier than she learned to talk and tell me her wants and needs, and, as time went on, it became easier for us both.

At a very early age, I taught Glennis to extend her arms over my arm, also extended, and it became easy to pick her up.

Our other key to family success was having a daily routine and sticking to it. We planned family meals and social engagements so that we didn't eat dinner late and were able to have Glennis home in bed at the usual time. After five months of staying at home with her and working part-time, I chose to return to work full-time, keep my part-time job and place her in day care.

Glennis liked going to day care. She learned to socialize and was never bored being around other children. I never once regretted the decision to place her there.

Chapter 16
Wyoming Bound

A year after Glennis was born, I became pregnant again. Joe and I both wanted another child, our goal being two children, and I was hoping for a boy. This pregnancy was different for me. It was so much more tiring having one child to supervise plus working full-time for half the duration of the pregnancy. I could not rest when I felt the need, since Glennis' wants were constantly on my mind.

I worked as a chief flight instructor for a Part 141 flight school. While performing those duties, I also managed the daily operations of the flight school. I scheduled maintenance on our "fleet" of five aircraft, did stage checks for students at various levels of training and recurrent training for flight instructors on staff, assigned new students, talked to prospective customers interested in flight training and kept the books.

To execute the duties of chief flight instructor, it was necessary for me to ride with the FAA for a third time. The first ride was for my private certificate, the second time was for my second class medical certificate. The third was to be the Part 141 Chief Flight Instructor checkride. There was no way I could objectively prepare for the ride. There were no published guidelines, as there are for other ratings, to bone up on. There was an oral exam followed by a practical exam in the C-172.

The check ride started out with a two-hour oral on the Federal Aviation Regulations, Parts 141, 91 and 61 (governing flight training). After the oral, the remainder of the checkride was postponed, not because I did not know the FARs, but because the inspector felt I did not know the day-to-day flight school operations.

The checkride was continued a week later with a different inspector, and it started with a four-hour oral exam. Then, that afternoon, I postponed the practical checkride due to thunderstorms in the Louisville and airport vicinity.

Several weeks later the ride was given to me by yet a third inspector, who was observed by his supervisor as he gave the oral exam to me. The flight was one and a half hours long, and I was finally done. I had passed! I was relieved. I never knew it would be such an ordeal, or a complete test and review of my flight-instructor knowledge. I doubt I will want to be a chief flight instructor without the help of published guidelines. The checkride was unnecessarily long, and I felt over scrutinized. I thought having one arm had something to do with it.

I liked the job managing the flight school. For the first time, I used both my previous management and flying experience. After assuming the responsibility for daily operations, I soon became aware that the school was very deep in debt. It owed for previous maintenance done on the training aircraft, and the present overhead expenses exceeded monthly income. I strived to reduce costs in all areas. I worked with airframe and powerplant mechanics, purchased my own parts and had a mechanic's helper work on aircraft needing repairs or inspections — with close supervision from the airframe and powerplant mechanic.

My efforts were too little too late, however, and the flight school closed in January 1991. I was asked to continue on with the new owner of the school, but after a month of transition, the new owner chose not to have an on-site manager. From February until May, I continued as a part-time flight instructor.

Four short months later, on May 26, 1991, Hattie Amelia Marshall was born. Glennis took to her immediately; there was no adjustment for her but an immense one for me. Suddenly, it was not like having another child but like having four children. The requirements of both small children, as I once feared, was physically demanding. Again, my mother came from Southern California to Louisville to help with Hattie's homecoming and care. Hattie was a precious infant.

A month later, Joe and I decided we could no longer afford to have him work only part-time, flying as first officer on a Citation jet for a local corporation in Louisville. So he accepted a full-time position with a small commuter airline operating out of Provo, Utah. Alpine Air offered a fleet of Beech 99s and Piper Navajo Chieftains. Joe's job was to nightly fly freight in a Chieftain from Evanston, Wyoming, to Rock Springs, then on to Denver, overnight there, then return via the same route the next morning. Many changes happened abruptly.

We leased our home in Louisville and arranged to move my mobile home from Billings, Montana, to Wyoming. In the back of our minds we hoped for a rapid return to the

Louisville area. When Hattie was barely a month old, we packed up necessary belongings and moved across country, 1,500 miles west to Evanston, Wyoming.

I was surprised to see Evanston was mostly high desert. The landscape offered rolling hills with generous amounts of sage brush and the majestic Uinta mountains to the south. Wildlife was abundant with antelope grazing on the high plain areas and deer encroaching on the town.

After getting settled, I worked to find employment for myself and suitable day care for Hattie and Glennis. I applied for and received certification from the Department of Education to substitute teach in the public schools. I was soon employed several days a week. After six months of teaching at the high school level, I became disenchanted with the lack of interest on the part of students. I found it became a constant discipline problem in the classroom rather than students desiring to learn.

During the same time I taught in the public schools, I taught an open pottery workshop through the local community college extension. Additionally, I had a few private students who wanted to learn to fly in the challenging weather of southwest Wyoming.

While I juggled three part-time jobs, I took the primary responsibility for raising the girls. It was so taxing for me to manage the household, work and take care of them. It seemed there were never enough hours in the day to get everything done. I had trouble keeping the house tidy. As soon as I picked up toys, the girls were back tossing the toys out of the box. Laundry seemed to multiply by itself. Hattie did not sleep through the night, waking up every hour or two to eat. I became a walking zombie.

As I had learned in the past, the hard way, I had to simplify my life and let some things go. (More on this in Part II of this book.) I had to relax my standards for cleanliness. I tried, though, to keep the living room neat in case of an unexpected visitor. It seemed as if I was never done with household chores. Yet, I wanted to spend as much time with the Glennis and Hattie as I could. I was constantly striving for balance. I decided I would make a point of reading to Glennis each night before bed and playing with Hattie so each had quality time alone with me. I made them my priority and worked my schedule around them. Nothing was perfect, but it didn't matter; I had the rest of my life to clean house. I was aware that the girls were growing quickly, and I only had a short time with them while they were little and impressionable.

After living several months in Evanston, Joe, still with Alpine, was checked out in a Beech 99 as a back-up captain; he could start building the all-important turbine time in preparation for an airline position. After months of pestering, I finally landed a job working with the local FBO, Star West, managing the flight training program, flying low-level pipeline patrol and single-engine charter. One of my new manager's concerns at Star West was how the paying charter customers would view my missing arm. He discussed this with me; we agreed it would have to be addressed. I suggested that I handle it on an individual basis with the inquisitive customer. To my relief most passengers did more curious watching than asking.

A month and a half after securing my dream job at Star West, Joe was told in late May 1992 that Alpine Air had lost the contract to fly overnight mail from Evanston to Denver.

At that time, Joe was offered another position flying overnight mail in a Beech 99 from Gillette, Wyoming, to Rapid City, South Dakota, to Denver each night. Joe decided to take the new position. It would mean relocating to Gillette, Wyoming, in less than week's time.

I was devastated. I had the perfect job as a pilot with Star West, had worked nearly a year in an attempt to secure it, and now it came down to a mutual career choice. If Joe didn't take the new job offer from Alpine, he was out of both work and an opportunity for further turbine hours. We knew we could not make ends meet on my income, so we had no choice but to relocate to Gillette.

The next day, after jointly deciding upon the new position, the four of us hopped into a rented C-172 and flew up to Gillette for a few days to inspect our surroundings. Our primary task was to find a suitable mobile home park.

I had been to Gillette, Wyoming, before, but it was during less-than-desirable circumstances. The thought of living there, though, plagued me. What if local individuals remembered me from the airplane accident? How was I going to obtain work as a flight instructor?

On schedule and less than a week later, we moved the mobile home, complete with all our worldly belongings, to Gillette. We were fortunate to find a mobile-home park north of town, only three miles from the airport. As an added bonus, the park was surrounded by vast areas of open land used only for cattle grazing. We set to work getting ourselves settled, and Joe started his freight run in the Beech 99. He was looking forward to flying the Beech, which he felt was a safer aircraft to operate over mountainous terrain.

During the year he flew the Navajo from Evanston to

Denver, he managed to successfully deal with an intentional gear-up landing, after only the nose gear and one main gear extended, and one engine failure over Colorado's prominent Front Range. Turbine engines are known for their reliability. Knowing this was a relief for me, as well.

About two weeks after we moved to Gillette, I was checked out in both a Cessna 172 and 182 by the owner of the local FBO and began to teach. I involved myself again with the Wyoming chapter of the 99s and became an accident prevention counselor for the FAA. My voluntary role as a counselor provided me with opportunity to speak openly to pilots regarding all aspects of aviation safety without the pilots having to fear a citation or formal reprimand. I rekindled my interest in making bridal veils for a local shop and dedicated myself to the children.

Hattie, now a year old, and Glennis, nearly three, are more than a full-time job for me most days. I dearly love them both, enjoy seeing their daily changes, their individual learning processes, and communicating with them. I do have days, though, when I get frustrated. With both of them making demands on me, a typical day as a housewife and mother goes like this . . .

I get out of bed at 7:30 after Hattie arises, change her diaper, get Glennis up, feed them both breakfast, clean up the resulting mess, feed myself, put breakfast items away. Get the girls dressed, myself dressed, vacuum, straighten the girls' room, my room, start a load of laundry, fold laundry, go on errands, such as to the grocery store, and get back by lunchtime. Feed the girls, then myself, get Hattie to bed for a nap, clean up the lunch mess, think about the dinner meal, dry and fold more laundry, play with Glennis, take her for a walk, bike ride or swim while Joe is napping with Hattie. Straighten the kitchen while Glennis takes a nap, and by then Hattie is up, prepare the dinner meal, then Glennis is up, feed all four of us, clean up after the meal, clean the kitchen, then run a load of dishes in the dishwasher. Joe leaves for his nightly freight run, the girls go into the tub for a supervised bath. I get them dried them off and dressed for bed, and, meanwhile, I complete the laundry while they play together. I play with Hattie before she goes to bed, then read to Glennis before it is time for her to go to bed. After both children are in bed, I take a shower and wind down for an hour or less. By 10:00 at night I fall into bed – exhausted.

The thought dawned on me that perhaps it takes longer for me to complete any given task than it does a normal individual with two arms. Granted, I struggle putting diapers on, with squirmy Hattie. Getting her dressed, including putting on her shoes, can be trying at best. I am encouraged, though, at how well Glennis is dressing herself now and helping me with care of Hattie. Glennis will get a diaper, wipes, bottle, or toy for Hattie at my request. It *is* getting easier.

Still, there is not a day that goes by, while attending the children, that I wish I had two arms. Everything would be so much easier instead of a constant battle. Among all the frustrating situations which I try to ignore, there is one that I recall that causes me to laugh at myself.

One day we were hurrying to get out of the house to go on a few family errands. In my haste, I accidentally slammed the locked front door with my right coat sleeve partially inside. Instantly, allowing my futility to outwardly show, I said in an angry tone of voice, "Oh damned! My sleeve is caught in the door!" Behind me stood darling, curious Glennis. She promptly repeated my foul language to Joe, who was impatiently waiting in the car. I thought then about future events and how I must set a better example for both my children.

A few months after we moved to Gillette, I had the courage to return to Recluse, the site of the airplane crash eight years earlier. Since we were living only 35 miles south of Recluse, I felt that it would be of interest to both Joe and me. Also, I wanted to thank Fred Oedekoven for being there during my time of need.

After arriving in Recluse that gray overcast day, and much to my surprise, I could not remember where the airport was located. Meanwhile, the thoughts of the terrifying crash kept flashing through my mind. Near town, I glanced to the left of the main road and saw a windsock. There was the infamous grass strip.

We drove across the embankment, the same one that the airplane had intensely struck with its tail. The berm of dirt was gone. Then we continued down the grass runway to the end. Joe, the girls and I got out of the car. I tried to explain to Joe what I remembered and what I had been told about the fateful chain of events leading up to the crash.

After our tour, we met with Fred, and I gave him a scrimshaw-engraved knife as a gift. It was good to meet him again — but under much better conditions this time. Really, I thought, I don't know how or what I could possibly give someone who helped to save my life. We discussed the crash in detail and how lucky he thought Bud, Julie, Bill and I were to have lived through it. During our ride home to Gillette, I was pensive yet thankful I had so much to live for.

Chapter 17
Future Plans

M y most immediate goal has been writing this book. I am determined to get this information to individuals suffering a recent loss of a limb or the loss of *use* of a limb (as in stroke/head injury cases). I am encouraging other disabled individuals to write about their trials. Writing allowed me to purge myself of pent-up hostility and anger, and buried emotions which surfaced. At the onset of this project, I was not aware that its writing would be a psychological benefit.

I would like to have funds available to buy an airplane and fly myself around the United States to help those individuals in some way to cope with their loss of a limb. I would like to get involved with promoting disabled group causes; to promote ideas that are currently surfacing, such as the use of more disabled actors in movie and stage productions; to help achieve easier access, leading to complete access, for wheelchair-bound people; and to contribute to equality in job hiring for the impaired.

Most importantly, however, I want to assist in changing the way the general, "whole," able-bodied public views a disability. This can be done through exposure, experience

The Marshall family ice skating in Evanston, Wyoming, December, 1991.

and education. Specifically, speaking, getting disabilities out in the open, and allowing the general public to gain experience working with impaired individuals on any level will help to change public opinion. Education and widespread media coverage helps to promote disabled causes, as well.

As for my personal future goals, I would like to learn to

water ski; but, so far, the right set of circumstances and learning environment has not presented itself on a consistent basis. I have tried to water ski but have invariably had trouble holding on to the tow rope. It seems I just don't have the strength in my arm to pull my body out of the water. As for my aviation career, there are several areas I may pursue. Areas which might be open to me include the airlines, corporate flying, aviation management or government service. I would like to finish my college degree, not a complex goal, but one that I would need to set aside the time to complete. I would like to see ElectricBride flourish. The idea, in my opinion, might be several years ahead of its time. I do want to spend maximum time with my children. I want to re-live my life through their lives, but be careful all the while not to seek my glory through them. I feel I have had plenty of glory myself. I do want to see Joe's aviation career progress, either to a corporate or an airline position. We would like to travel the world extensively together and with our children.

Part II

How One Does It

Chapter 18
Nine Helpful Steps to Recovery

T he next three chapters provide recovery information for the reader. If you, or someone you love or care for, have recently suffered a loss of a limb, or the use of a limb, I offer the following advice:

1. *Save your energy.* Until you make adjustments to your new situation, which will not be overnight, you will need to pace yourself. Sit down to do a task rather than stand up. Complete tasks requiring physical exertion upon arising; save the mental tasks for later in the day.

2. *Set and achieve small goals.* This pertains to all aspects of your altered life style. From the smallest of goals — for example — tying your shoes or preparing a meal, remember to keep it simple. Build on your skills. Later on, after daily tasks are mastered and a routine is easier, set larger goals. I define a larger goal as driving a car or resuming a career.

3. *Plan outings carefully.* Consolidate trips; don't overdo it. For example, I suggest you attempt a trip to the grocery store, return home, and do nothing else physically demanding that day. In my case, I often elect to get everything, such as food and sundries at the grocery store. Even though some items cost slightly more, that is one less trip to another location. Don't forget that your body will be physically trying to compensate for the loss, but your mind will want to continue as before.

4. *Resume relationships.* See your friends and continue prior activities. Some adjustments may be necessary for your physical change. Have your friends and loved ones help you rethink how you can continue these mutually satisfying physical activities. Your friends and loved ones will become even more dear to you and you to them.

5. *Seek professional assistance.* Don't be shy about pursuing physical therapists, psychologists, prosthetic designers, and physicians who are genuinely interested in your well being. Recovery from a physical loss is too demanding to completely manage by yourself.

6. *Join a support group.* Get involved with others who are dealing with a similar set of circumstances. You will be able to exchange information, discuss various techniques to complete tasks more efficiently, participate in group activities

and make new friends. Contact your local hospital or orthopedic clinic.

7. *Start a new relationship.* If you are without a partner, having someone special in your life is a major advantage. Don't be embarrassed about your impairment. Actually, I have found it to be a blessing. From the beginning of my relationship with my husband, Joe, I found him unaffected by my lack of an arm. My husband saw beyond my physical looks to my inner beauty. When I was single, looking for male companionship, I finally realized that men attracted to me were not shallow. They truly appreciated and enjoyed my talents and personality. They admired my savvy.

8. *Go shopping.* Psychologically, spending money on myself is the best therapy. If you are a recent arm amputee, you too may want to reconsider your present wardrobe. Perhaps clothing styles which would include easier access would better suit your needs. In my case, I chose not to wear sleeveless blouses or swim wear which exposes what is left of my right arm. Yes, it is my own hangup to cover my arm, but it is what makes *me* the most comfortable.

9. *Go on with your life.* Don't let a loss of this nature set you back. Refuse pity, don't dwell on your loss. Don't listen to nay sayers who tell you, "it isn't possible," whatever "it" might be. You may be-

come mentally depressed and feel life is not worth living, but there are always things to be thankful for. Over the years I have turned to family, friends, work, physical and creative activities to discourage depression from overtaking me. Stay busy. Try something new, take a risk, don't be afraid of the outcome. Remember to be patient and determined, work hard and remain persistent. You can have anything you want out of life.

Chapter 19
Helpful Ideas for Daily Living

I f you have recently lost the use of an arm, or are a recent arm amputee, this next section will be a convenient reference for you regarding day-to-day tasks. Not only have I offered advice on routine tasks, but information I felt would be helpful in other areas, as well.

Kitchen & Cooking

1. *Pace yourself.* Remember, your first priority is to conserve movement and energy, minimize standing and, if necessary, take frequent short breaks. You may need to relax for five minutes each hour, then resume your activity. I have found that I can continue at a specific activity longer if I pace myself throughout the day.

2. *Shorten your day.* Decide on a menu, for example, a week at a time and plan a very careful shopping list. I have one grocery store I normally shop. For this particular grocery store, I have compiled my shopping list to exactly match the store layout.

This way I waste no precious steps. I try to shop the day before my weekly planned menu starts.

Trying to grocery shop and cook in the same day can often be overwhelming to me, especially if I am entertaining. For meal preparation on the day I shop, I stick to something that is quick to fix. I am not embarrassed to make my family something out of the frozen section or even go out to eat. If you stop to analyze grocery shopping, there is a considerable amount of effort that is required. Planning, organizing, actual physical exertion in the form of driving to and from the store, shopping, then unloading groceries at home and putting them away in the pantry or refrigerator.

3. *Cook simply.* From my days as a food service manager, I always try to use a standardized recipe at home for consistent results. This refers to a consistent time frame as well. You want to know, before you begin, the time it takes to prepare a meal or, at least the main course, which can be the most time consuming. Using a standardized recipe each time does not mean you cannot add your own special touches. I try to pick simple, easy recipes that incorporate fresh ingredients.

4. *Organize your kitchen.* When preparing a meal, assemble all your ingredients first — mixing bowls, pots, pans, a sharp vegetable peeler, measuring cups and spoons, a cutting board and a chef's

knife. The key to your success is a very sharp knife. I prefer an eight-inch chef's knife for small chopping jobs.

Don't be shy about using helpful kitchen tools, such as an egg separator, electric can opener, bottle opener, stationary mixer or a food processor. If you are having difficulty grating cheese without the assistance of a food processor, you can purchase a variety of cheeses already grated. For years I struggled to grate cheese using either a flat or square metal grater. Seeing that I was having difficulty in this area, a close friend, Tom Crooks, made me a wooden box-like device that allowed a flat grater to slide in horizontally. It held the grater snugly so I could push the block of cheese against it. The holder was designed in such a way to permit the cheese to fall below the grater and into an empty space. Now I use a food processor almost exclusively for grating, chopping or fine slicing.

5. *Removing lids. When* opening vacuum-packed glass items, such as juice, pickles, or baby food, use an ice pick to punch a small hole in the lid to relieve the pressure difference. Then the lid can be easily removed.

6. *Cutting vegetables.* Round fruits and vegetables will need to be cut so they have a flat side before you can work with them. If necessary, use a clean,

Peeling a potato using a paring knife. Note that the potato stays in place better when cut in half and placed flat side down on the cutting board.

damp towel to keep fruits and vegetables from sliding around while you are working with them. Though I rarely peel carrots, the wet towel idea works well. I have also scrubbed carrots after being placed on a damp towel, with a flat, nylon pad that is usually used for cleaning pans. You may find small, baby carrots at your grocery store which are already peeled. These type of carrots are fine for soups or stews, but may not make the best carrot sticks for a relish tray. Potatoes are another story. I find trying to peel them, even after they have been cut to lay flat on a cutting board, very difficult. As an alternative, I either leave the skin on and select recipes that allow that choice, such as new-red-potato salad, or I will cut the potato in half, then use the paring knife to carve off the skin. This is slightly more wasteful than peeling but much easier.

7. *Washing dishes.* During cleanup, if you do not have an automatic dishwasher, then I suggest you use a plastic (Rubbermaid-type) dish tub, placed in the sink, which helps keep the dishes from sliding around while you scrub them. If food is stubborn about being removed, then pre-soaking may be your simplest option. I keep close at hand a sponge that has on one side to wipe up spills and on the other side a nylon scrubber. If I want to clean off a knife blade, I can press down on the sponge/scrubber, with nylon scrub side up, and clean the blade.

8. *Protecting your skin.* My hand and fingers are sacred to me; they do everything for me and members of my family. I cannot take the chance of cutting or injuring my hand, so I am always careful with sharp or hot objects and use a glove for cleaning. I would suggest you do the same and continually be aware of possible safety hazards in the kitchen area. Pace yourself so you are not rushed. Injure yourself, and you're out of commission!

Going Out to Eat a Meal

1. *Cutting meat.* You may think twice about ordering a steak, or other whole pieces of meat, that will
require using a knife to cut. It can be an awkward
situation unless you ask the waiter to have your
steak cut up in the kitchen before it is served to
you. Or if someone is present at the table with you
who can cut it up, that will suffice. But I like the
first method better. It is important to me to eat
food immediately after it is served, when it is at
peak temperature. Having someone at the table
cut a steak causes delay. Often, I order a kabob,
which is usually presented in small, bite-sized
pieces over rice, or a chicken or fish item, which
I can cut with the side of my fork. I often joke that
I do not want to eat anything anyway that I can't
cut with a fork. When I am asked where I might
like to eat, I often opt for Chinese food, because
most dishes are prepared in bite-size pieces. In any
setting, I am not hesitant to ask my waiter for
assistance so I can have a pleasant dining experience.

2. *Serving yourself.* Buffets can often be a problem
because you will be required to somehow position
your plate securely while you place food on it.
Depending on the buffet set-up, there may be
room to place your plate on the buffet line next to
a food item, then serve yourself that food item. I
have also asked restaurant personnel for their
assistance in holding the plate as I moved along

the line. In a salad bar situation, I have asked waitresses, on occasion, to make me a garden salad – which they will gladly do – rather than hassle with the salad bar. I have always managed to be self-sufficient but at the same time have avoided situations which may call attention to my impairment. But remember that it's always okay to ask for help.

Cleaning/Household Chores

1. *Scrubbing.* Unfortunately, cleaning house is a fact of life. I already mentioned wearing latex gloves while using harsh cleaning agents. I could never allow the skin on my hand to be chafed or get so dry it would crack. Now you can't either. Save as many steps as you can by confining cleaning tasks to one area in the house at a time. For example, clean the entire bathroom at one time instead of each area; that is, clean the tub or sink on separate occasions. Carry cleaning supplies in a caddie that can be easily transported from one room to another.

2. *Ironing.* For me, ironing clothes is drudgery. It is difficult to securely keep clothing on the ironing board so the weight of the clothing doesn't pull it off the board surface. In the past, I have used straight pins to fasten an unruly clothing item to the ironing board pad so I could iron the fabric. I

try to sit down to iron, and I thereby save my energy.

Again, I do my best to be self-sufficient, but I have resorted to sending my husband's all-cotton shirts out to be laundered. Ironing them became too time consuming and frustrating. Because ironing became a task I hated, I reduced my workload by letting go my standards somewhat. I chose to not iron sheets, pillow cases and other linen items. My cotton dresses were sent out to be laundered along with Joe's shirts. I purchased clothing items which did not require ironing after removal from the dryer or, at the most, only a touch up.

As a reminder, use caution to avoid contact with the heated iron. Please understand I am not being parental about your impairment, but you must take care of what you have remaining. Hot irons cause burns on the hand and fingers which are not only troublesome or impossible to bandage, but the recovery from a burn is long and painful.

Household Helps

1. *"Convenience" tables.* In my home I have a small table positioned on both sides of the front door entrance. The tables allow me to set groceries, as an example, at the door, while I use my keys to unlock the door. I am able to set one child on the

table, then I do not have to strain my back to bend over and pick up the weight of the child at ground level. This may seem trivial, but reducing the frequency of pulling 25 pounds up off the ground decreased the occurrence of one-sided back aches and paralyzing stiff necks.

Bath & Grooming

1. *Safety.* If you have recently lost an arm, your balance may be off; be careful in the bathtub and/ or shower. Be patient with your new situation; reposition bathroom handrails to the most easily accessible position, if necessary.

2. *Shaving.* Being female and wanting to shave both underarms myself, I initially used an electric razor; now I use a straight razor and shave in the shower. I have no problem raising my left arm, then curling my hand around with razor held firmly and reaching the armpit area to shave. I might suggest a safety mirror in the bathtub to assist you in seeing the top of your armpit so you can shave the area completely.

3. *Hair care.* Pick an easy, carefree hairstyle, perhaps a permed look. In the past I have been an advocate of both permed and straight hair styles, both long and short. If I wanted to curl my hair, I used an electric curling iron. I have never had

success with any type of hair rollers. They all seemed a two-handed project because they usually required me to hold my hair in place with the roller while I used pins or clips to keep them in place.

If you choose to curl your hair, select a curling iron that is the spring-loaded type – one that will hold a lock of hair firmly against the curling iron, while you roll the remainder around the shaft of the iron. Seeing the back of your head will require a wall mounted mirror so you can see to use the curling iron in this area. It takes practice to be good at using the iron in order to produce satisfying results.

4. *Cosmetics.* The use of cosmetics is an individual preference that does not take two hands to apply – just practice.

5. *Nail care.* Having painted nails made people curious enough to ask me how I did it by myself. Nail polish can be applied by dipping the brush in the polish with your hand, put the plastic applicator in your mouth, hold your fingers still and let the motion of your head paint your nails. This trick takes some practice.

I always hold my breath while polishing each nail; the smell is offensive to me and the fumes can be toxic and flammable. To remove the polish, you can use the traditional method of pouring a small

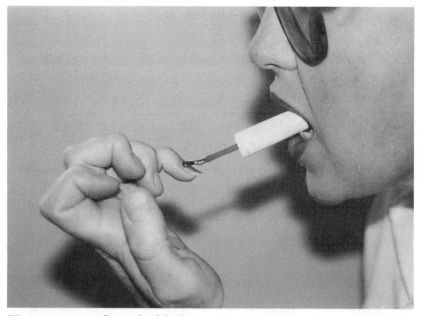

Use your teeth to hold the nail polish brush, and let the motion of your head paint your nails.

amount of remover on a tissue, then use your thumb to do most of the work, pressing the remover soaked tissue against each nail.

You may want to use the new type of nail polish remover with a sponge enclosed. This allows you to rub your nail directly on the chemical-soaked sponge, which is enclosed in a plastic container, removing all traces of polish. When filing my nails to an appealing shape, I use an emery board and hold it securely between my knees. Then I keep my fingers ridged next to the emery board, while I move my hand.

Jewelry

1. *Earrings.* I noticed years ago that the best-looking earrings seemed to be of the pierced variety. Not wanting to limit myself to the clip style, I had my ears pierced. Some types of backings worked better than others; I prefer the large, disk-type backing, usually used for large, fashion earrings. I find these work the best for small- or large-style earrings.

   To put on a typical earring I use two motions; I put the earring post through my ear first. Then I pick up the earring's back and use my middle finger to hold the front of the earring, then use my thumb and first finger to put the earring backing in place.

2. *Necklaces.* About any type of clasp for a necklace works fairly well one-handed, except the type that requires you to screw the two sides together. If the necklace is of the screw variety and the clasp is long enough, you can watch in the mirror while you insert one side of the clasp in-between your teeth to hold it in place, then use your hand to twist the remaining side together.

   If your necklace is the typical loop-to-loop type, the best thing to do is move the small loop as far to the front of your neck as you can. Then watch in the mirror and use your thumb and first finger to open the large loop and fasten the two loops

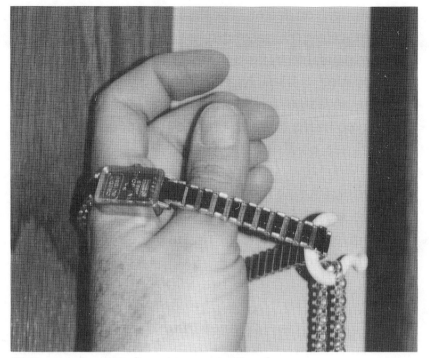

Put on your watch using a cup hook.

together. If you have a string of pearls with a hook-type clasp, for example, follow the same procedure as the loop-to-loop type.

3. *Wristwear.* I do not generally wear bracelets, because I have found they have a tendency to get in the way of my busy hand. If you chose to wear a bracelet, wear the hoop type. I hold the bracelet between my knees and push my hand through the hoop. If the bracelet is the type that fastens with a clasp, it is impossible for me to place it on my wrist without assistance. I do wear a watch, and have had success getting two types of watch band

designs on and off. The first is an expandable-type bracelet, the second is a large-clasp type. The expandable, by far being the easier, can be wrapped around a hook to place on my wrist and also removed quickly in that manner. The large-clasp type needs the assistance of my mouth to get it closed, so it's not my favorite.

4. *Rings*. A ring (on the traditional ring finger) can be easily worn by using your middle and ring finger to help slide the ring in place. Removal is in the same fashion.

Wallpapering

It occurred to me that you may want to wallpaper; it could be a personal challenge to you, for no other reason (so you, too, can be a one-armed paperhanger). Though I wrote in previous chapters about my wallpapering success, you may want to refer to this outline, instead.

1. *Paper selection*. Select a wallpaper that is not too thick, such as a vinyl. But use a paper with vinyl coating, pre-pasted, with an overall and short repeat pattern.

2. *Equipment selection*. Invest in the right tools and equipment — a water tray in which to soak the paper to activate the paste (but you can also use the bathtub, if it is more convenient), a sharp,

razor-type cutter with break-away blades, a clean, damp sponge, a seam roller if you desire, a yardstick or metal tape for measuring, a steady ladder and a chalk line plumb. The secret to completing any project is first having all the right tools to do the job.

3. *Wall preparation.* Don't forget to use wallpaper preparation on the walls before going ahead with your project. This will insure that the paper will adhere to the wall surface until you decide to remove it at a later date.

4. *Marking plumb lines.* Be sure to use the chalk plumb line to mark a straight line from ceiling to floor. This line will be your guide, so the wallpaper will hang straight on the wall. This is probably the secret to making your project look professional.

To start my chalk line, I mark a specific distance from the corner at the ceiling level, then hang my chalk line from that spot. (More times than not, even in the most professionally built homes, the walls are not perfectly straight at the corner.) For example, let's say the width of your wallpaper is 24 inches, I start my plumb line 22 inches from the corner. This allows me to continue the paper around the inside corner for two inches. Then my next piece of wallpaper can overlap the existing two inches into the corner, giving the wall a finished look.

5. *Getting started.* If you are left handed, start from right to left, so you can use your arm to help hold the paper in place while you use your wrist to smooth the paper to your right side. The opposite is true, if you have your right hand. The secret to getting started is to glue a portion of the paper to the wall — enough so it will hold the weight of the remaining paper hanging below. Then, line the rest of the paper up with the chalk line and adjust the portion of the paper up to the chalk line that was holding the weight of the entire strip.

Driving

1. *Take it easy.* You probably are new to driving with one arm, and I suggest you take your time relearning how to drive.

2. *Make it easy.* Use a car with an automatic transmission that reduces the workload and amount of concentration required to get from point A to point B. If you already have a car with a manual transmission, use it. But remember, during the times you are shifting, your hand cannot be simultaneously on the steering wheel. This takes some planning ahead and getting used to. Downshift into a lower gear *before* you get to a corner. Use your knee to help you keep the car straight while you shift gears. If you wish to drive a car with manual transmission, you must have a car in good

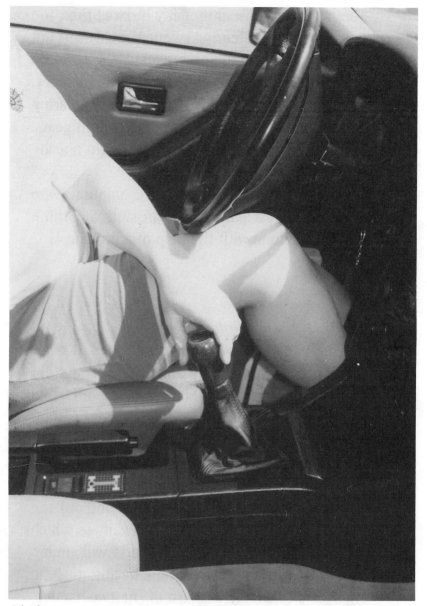

Shifting requires planning and practice.

condition, one that doesn't want to pull to either side. Pulling to either side could happen for a number of reasons: improperly inflated tires, too much play in the steering mechanism, wheels out of alignment or grabbing brakes. Make sure the car will travel straight ahead without assistance. Though I do use my knee to hold the steering wheel in place while I use my hand to shift gears, I still require that my car tracks straight ahead.

3. *Get some help.* If you are a leg amputee who wishes to drive a manual transmission car, I think it could be done with the help of a prosthesis.

Child Care

1. *Choosing equipment.* Again, having the right equipment will make taking care of your child easier with one arm. There are a number of infant and children items on the market, some of which require *three* hands to operate; these items are frustrating to someone with two hands. I visited a children's store and spent time trying out the various models of high chairs, for example, which are available. Relatives and friends will understand why you are not accepting the antique high chair or crib simply because of the two-handed, and often stubborn or impossible, operation.

2. *Deciding on diapers.* If you chose to use cloth diapers, as I did for my first child, having a diaper

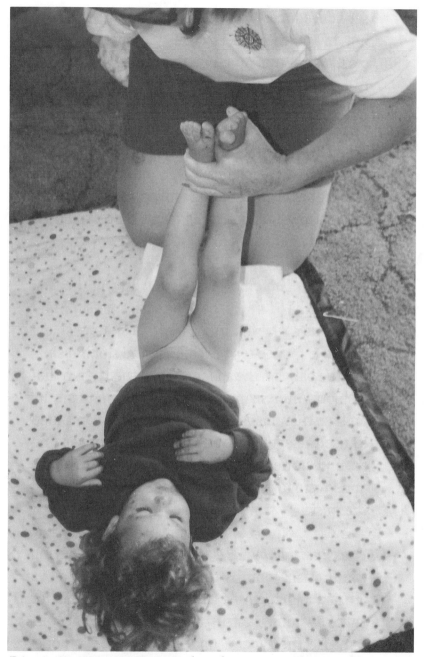

Diapering Hattie is simple when I use disposable wrap-arounds with self-stick tape closures.

service reduces the workload of the endless washing of soiled diapers. Use a diaper-wrap-type plastic pant that opens up flat to allow the diaper to be inserted and which then fastens with Velcro™ closures. Disposable diapers are the most convenient and easiest for me to use, though there are environmental considerations to keep in mind. I understand a child can use up to 2,000 disposable diapers before they are toilet trained. But the runoff from washing 2,000 cloth diapers should be considered, too.

3. *Bathing a baby.* Bathing a baby during the first few months of life can be done easily in a sink, and if you have that luxury, one with a sloping side. I placed a sponge-type cushion in the sloping sink, put the baby on the sponge and bathed her in that fashion. After six months she was able to sit up, and we then moved to the bath tub. I continued to use the sponge to keep the child from sliding around, however. At about nine months, the baby and I were taking showers together. That worked the best.

4. *Dressing a baby.* Dressing a baby is easy during the first six months because they do not move around much. Insist on clothes that zipper or snap; buttons are frustrating and time consuming. Use the type of undershirt that is kimono-style with snaps — no ties. Over-the-head type shirts are annoying, especially when the child is

not yet old enough to sit up without help.

Shoes with Velcro™ closures are fastest to operate for everyday wear, though for the baby I have used dressier shoes with buckle-type closures. Though I can manage shoes that tie, it is more difficult, especially if the baby squirms. Socks are a bit troublesome for me; they are small and going on a small foot! What worked best for me the first six months was to keep the baby in a "sleep and play" suit, for everyday activities, which enclosed the feet.

After she was able to sit up in a high chair, I dressed the baby's feet after breakfast was over, while she was still confined. That way the baby was not going anywhere and was unable to squirm away from me while I put on socks and shoes. Another key to success is to teach your child from day one to "push" their feet or hands through a pant leg or sleeve. After three months, the child will help you get her dressed by extending a firm arm or leg.

Sewing

1. *Buttons.* Sewing buttons onto a garment can prove to be laborious because it is difficult to hold the button in place to get started. I have used clear plastic tape to hold the button in the desired

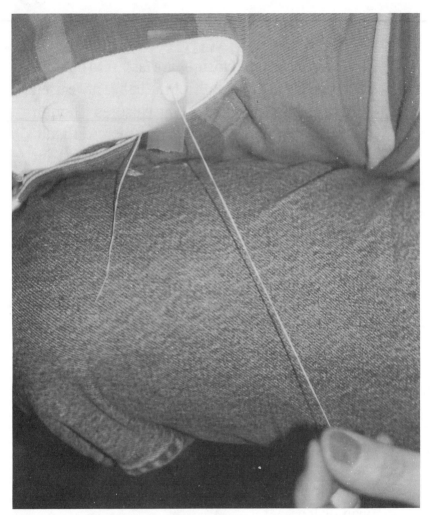

Sew on a button by holding the button in place with clear tape. Hold the shirt between your knees.

area and held the remainder of the garment securely between my knees. After you get the button thread started and have fastened the button with a few stitches, you can remove the tape and continue hand sewing until the button is attached. My sewing machine, which I prefer to use, will also sew on buttons, as do most newer machines.

2. *Projects.* If you chose to make sewing a hobby or wish to continue sewing, start with an easy project. Make placemats and napkins, or chose a simple dress pattern. Use sharp scissors to cut out your pattern and fabric. Use pins often and abundantly to affix pieces of cloth together before sewing. Follow step-by-step directions from the pattern manufacturer for the correct construction of your project. Start small, then work up to that tailored, wool-lined jacket with bound button holes.

3. *Difficult projects.* Try new craft projects or resume prior projects. You may have to re-think a one-handed method for holding a project so you can work on it. I have always used my knees, lips and/or teeth to temporarily hold items I am working on.

Clothing

1. *Simplicity first.* When selecting clothing, be sure it is something you can get on and off by yourself. For example, I don't purchase any dress with buttons down the back. I stick to pull-over-the-head-type dresses, those that zipper in the front or back, or button down the front.

For daily, casual wear, I like polo shirts, blue jeans, cotton rag socks, tie-type athletic shoes and pullover sweaters. For office wear, oxford blouses that button up the front and skirts that have an elastic waist or small zipper on the side or back for easy access. I wear a regular bra with front or back closure and fasten the bra first, in the same manner as it is to be worn. Then I put the garment over my head, slip my arm through the strap and adjust it in the proper position. I struggle to get panty hose on. I guess this is because it is a continuous fight against the elastic-type mesh from the ankles up to the waist.

Growing up, I watched two-handed girls gather each leg of the hose into a neat, compact tube in which they inserted their toe, then pulled the nylon mesh up their leg. I realized this was a delicate and impossible task. I could not gather my nylon mesh into a tube-like pile. My only choice was to carefully insert my foot into each leg, individually, then pull each side of the nylon up each leg a little at a time.

2. *Tying shoes.* My mother taught me to tie my shoes when I was six, during a road trip to Canada. For miles, she carefully thought about how she might use only one hand to tie her shoes. I watched as she analyzed every motion. I was entertained while watching her attempt to keep one hand from trying to help the other. Since I learned to tie my

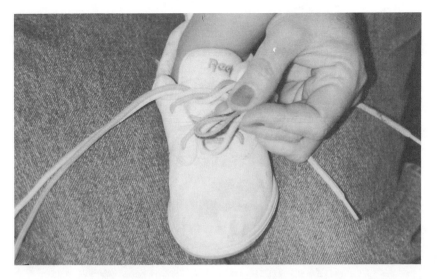

Step One: After adjusting shoe tightness, make a loop with one side of the laces, and hold it in place with your third finger.

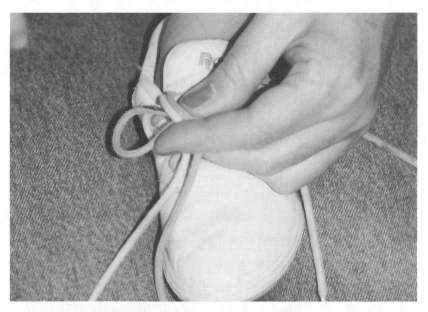

Step Two: With your free fingers, take the remaining shoe lace and wrap it around the loop.

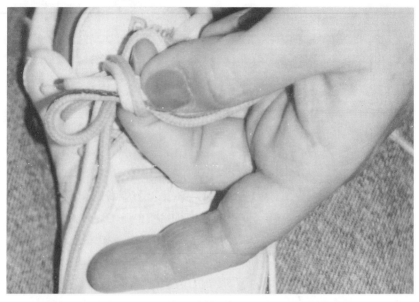

Step Three: Using your middle finger, push the remaining lace through, making the other side of the bow.

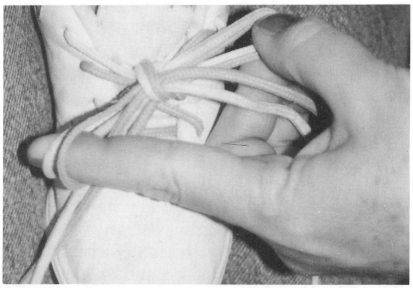

Step Four: Insert your first finger through one side of the bow and hold the other side with your thumb and middle finger, and pull at the same time to tighten the bow.

shoes at that age, I have showed curious individuals, throughout the years, how it is done. First, it helps to have shoe laces that are the cotton type with a texture, rather than slick, thin, nylon laces. Adjust the shoe tightness by pulling on both laces at the same time. Next, cross one lace over the other. Step on one side of the laces, while you pull the other with your hand, until you reach desired tension. Make a loop with one side of the laces and hold it in place with your third finger. With your free fingers, take the remaining lace and wrap it around the loop. Using your middle finger, push the remaining lace through, making the other side of the bow. Insert your first finger through one side of the bow and hold the other side with your thumb and middle finger, and pull at the same time to tighten the bow.

Please understand, I cannot identify *all* areas in which you may have trouble adjusting from two-handed to one-handed.

Writing this section was particularly taxing for me since I have been impaired for most of my life and don't consciously think about day-to-day tasks being difficult. In addition, I have not written about areas that are essentially out of my league, such as using various types of hand tools, changing tires on a car or mechanically maintaining a car.

I have always had an attitude that allowed me to *try anything*. This included any procedure, any tool or device. If in doubt, *try it*. If you don't try it, you will never know if you can do it. If you should come across an area you feel I have not identified and with which I can help you, please write to me in care of the publisher, Rainbow Books, Inc., P. O. Box 430, Highland City, FL 33846-0430.

Chapter 20
Resources

This section offers addresses with telephone numbers, in many cases, of government agencies and other associations dedicated to helping you recover and rehabilitate after your loss. None are specifically recommended unless noted.

Department of Labor and Employment Security
Division of Vocational Rehabilitation
(see the U.S. Government listing in your local phone book, or contact your local Social Security office for a referral)
Evaluates individuals who have lost their jobs (or who cannot get a job) as a result of a physical, mental or emotional disability. Provides prosthetics, medications, surgery, and vocational and other education, *free of charge.*

U.S. Department of Education
Office of Special Education and Rehabilitative Services
Switzer Bldg., Room 3132
Washington, DC 20202-2524
Phone (202) 732-1241
Responds to inquiries about federally funded programs for

persons with disabilities and information on federal legisla-
tion affecting the disabled community.

American Amputee Foundation
Box 250218 Hillcrest Station
Little Rock, AR 72225
Phone (501) 666-2523
Provides free peer counseling to new amputees, and their
families, to aid in their adjustment to limb amputation.

Amputee Shoe & Glove Exchange
P. O. Box 27067
Houston, TX 77227
Free information exchange to facilitate swaps of unneeded
shoes and gloves by amputees.

National Association of the Physically Handicapped
Bethesda Scarlet Oaks, No. 117
440 Lafayette Ave.
Cincinnati, OH 45220-1000
Phone (513) 961-8040
Seeks to advance the social, economic and physical welfare
of the physically handicapped.

National Head Injury Foundation
1140 Connecticut Ave., NW
Ste. 812
Washington, DC 20036
Phone (202) 296-6443
Works to stimulate public awareness and improve the
quality of life for patients with head injury.

Handicapped SCUBA Association
7172 W. Stanford Ave.
Littleton, CO 80123
Is interested in advancing and promoting SCUBA diving among the handicapped.

National Handicapped Sports
4405 East-West Hwy.
Ste. 603
Bethesda, MD 20814
Promotes sports and recreation opportunities for individuals with physical disabilities.

Courage Stroke Network
c/o Courage Center
3915 Golden Valley Rd.
Golden Valley, MN 55442
Offers support services for individuals recovering from a stroke.

National Stroke Association
30-0 E. Hampden Ave.
Ste. 240
Englewood, CO 80110-2654

National Council on Independent Living
Troy Atrium
4th Street & Broadway
Troy, NY 12180
Offers programs to assist disabled individuals with housing, counseling and independent skills training.

About the Author

Not believing it couldn't be done, Sheri Coin Marshall, a right-arm, above-elbow amputee at age three, has always achieved the seemingly impossible. From the time she was a child through her adult life, she set and attained goals difficult for the two-handed. Undaunted as she tried her hand at riding and caring for a horse, she also learned to drive a manual transmission car, to race a high-performance drag boat, and to fly. Then, at age 27, tragedy struck again when she was involved as a passenger in a small airplane crash.

Escaping death, she fought back from a severe head injury. She developed a lighted bridal veil while recovering, and for her efforts was awarded a patent from the United States Commissioner of Patents and Trademarks. She resumed her aviation career and went on to become a Federal Aviation Administration Certified Flight Instructor and Airline Transport Pilot. She trained to be certified as a YMCA sports diver and flew to Alaska in a single-engine airplane. She met a professional pilot, fell in love and was married. She and her husband have two children.

Sheri managed to overcome demanding physical barriers to child care. And nearing her fortieth birthday, she pauses to look back at her incredible life. *One Can Do It* is not only a dynamic story, it will be an inspiration to anyone, physically impaired or not, *who won't take "no" for an answer.*

One Can Do It:
A How-to Guide for the Physically Handicapped
by Sheri Coin Marshall

For additional copies of *One Can Do It,* telephone TOLL FREE 1-800-356-9315. MasterCard/VISA/American Express accepted.

To order *One Can Do It* direct from the publisher, send your check or money order for $14.95 plus $3.00 shipping and handling ($17.95 postpaid) to Rainbow Books, Inc., P. O. Box 430, Highland City, FL 33846-0430.

For *quantity purchases,* telephone Rainbow Books, Inc., (813) 648-4420 or write to Rainbow Books, Inc., P. O. Box 430, Highland City, FL 33846-0430.